D0573144

CONTRIBUTORS

J. J. Brody
David M. Brugge
William B. Gillespie
W. James Judge
Robert H. Lister
William Lumpkins
Robert P. Powers
Polly Schaafsma
Douglas W. Schwartz
Michael Zeilik

New Light On Chaco Canyon

New Light On

SCHOOL OF AMERICAN RESEARCH PRESS

Chaco Canyon

PUEBLO BONITO
PREHISTORIC RUIN
CANYON NATIONAL MONUMENT
CHACO CANYON, N M
DWELLINGS WITH 800 ROOMS AND 32
UPIED FROM 919 A.D. TILL 1130 A.D.

Edited by David Grant Noble

An Issue of
EXPLORATION
the Annual Bulletin of the School of American Research

SCHOOL OF AMERICAN RESEARCH PRESS
Post Office Box 2188
Santa Fe, New Mexico 87504

DIRECTOR OF PUBLICATIONS: Jane Kepp
EDITORS: Laura de la Torre Bueno, Malinda Elliott
DESIGNER: Deborah Flynn
COMPOSITOR: Business Graphics
PRINTER: Paragon Press

Library of Congress Cataloging in Publication Data
Main entry under title:
New light on Chaco Canyon.

   "Special volume in the School of American Research
Exploration series"—Foreword.
   Bibliography: p. 91
   Includes index.
   1. Pueblo Indians—Antiquities—Addresses, essays,
lectures. 2. Indians of North America—New Mexico—
Chaco Canyon Region—Antiquities—Addresses, essays,
lectures. 3. Chaco Canyon Region (N.M.)—Antiquities—
Addresses, essays, lectures. 4. New Mexico—Antiqui-
ties—Addresses, essays, lectures. I. Noble, David
Grant. II. Exploration (Santa Fe, N.M.) Special number.
E99.P9N278   1984   978.9'82   84-10506
ISBN 0-933452-10-1 (pbk.)

Cover: series of doorways at Pueblo Bonito. Photo by David Noble, 1984.
Frontispiece: panoramic view of Pueblo Bonito and the Wetherill trading post.
Photo by Almeron Newman, 1940, courtesy National Park Service.

Contents

Acknowledgments

THE PUBLICATION of *New Light on Chaco Canyon* was supported by contributions from Charlotte N. Gray, the Inn at Loretto, and the Lounsbery Foundation. I sincerely thank these donors.

This book would not have been possible without the generous cooperation of its authors, and I would like to thank Jerry Brody, Dave Brugge, Bill Gillespie, Jim Judge, Bob Lister, Bill Lumpkins, Bob Powers, Polly Schaafsma, and Mike Zeilik. Others who assisted in the project include John D. Beal, Jim Bradford, Eleanor Herriman, Steven Lekson, Marsha Truell Newren, Steve Post, Cherie Scheick, and Richard B. Woodbury. I also appreciate the assistance of the Maxwell Museum of Anthropology at the University of New Mexico, the Museum of New Mexico's Laboratory of Anthropology and Photographic Archives, and the National Park Service.

DAVID G. NOBLE

Foreword

THERE IS a real mystery about Chaco Canyon, the kind on which archaeologists thrive. When I visited the canyon last fall after an absence of several years, my sensitivity to this special place was considerably heightened by a knowledge of the new explanations currently being proposed for many of the phenomena of Chacoan prehistory.

Driving north from Fence Lake toward the canyon, I was struck first by the starkness of the region. How was it possible that the most impressive prehistoric community in the Southwest was supported by this barren, dry landscape? As I continued up the unpaved washboard road, red cliffs gradually emerged around me. The late afternoon sun deepened the hue of the rocks, and long shadows intensified their ruggedness. Soon I found myself concentrating no longer on the place's desolation, but rather on its beauty.

Suddenly the canyon was there: huge cliffs bordering a flat valley bisected by a deep, straight-sided arroyo. As the sun dropped toward the horizon, the rocks' strong red contrasted with the soft tones of valley sand, sage, and grass. Within the arroyo were striking patches of green, the leaves of occasional giant cottonwoods fed by the intermittent waters of Chaco Wash. And dominating the upper section of the scene was that clear turquoise southwestern sky.

Dusk was rapidly closing in. I drove toward the ruins, but their high walls of local stone camouflaged them against the cliffs so successfully that I was nearly past them before they emerged to view. Yet approaching the great pueblos a thousand years ago, one would have seen the flickering lights of many fires, heard the sounds of human conversations and barking dogs, sensed the shadowed movements of the villages' inhabitants. During special times of year, the chanting and drumbeat of ritual dramas would have echoed off the cliffs.

I planned to visit these impressive greathouses, their huge kivas, and the remains of the prehistoric road system, and to peer through binoculars at the rocks on top of Fajada Butte for a glimpse of the ancient sun shrine there. But I had seen all of these places before, and my main purpose was to look at them through the new eyes provided by the most recent archaeological work at Chaco. This research has resulted in an explosion of knowledge about the canyon's unique culture and a wealth of new interpretations concerning how that culture came about.

Each era has had a different conception of Chaco Canyon's meaning. The Spanish and early American explorers saw the huge ruins as evidence first of Roman occupation, then of Aztec settlement. These first visitors could not conceive that anything so spectacular could have been created by the local Indians. Later, following the work of scholars like Bandelier in other areas of the Southwest, Chaco was thought to be the remains of a prehistoric Pueblo people who had lived only a short time prior to the Spanish entrada. In the 1930s the tree-ring dating method revealed the true age of these sites for the first time, and the knowledge that large pueblos had been constructed one thousand years ago added new wonder to their story. In the years before and after the Second World War, the research emphasis was on determining when people first arrived in the canyon and how their life there had changed through time. Finally, in the fifties, enquiry began to focus on why life in Chaco had evolved in a manner so distinct from developments in the rest of the Southwest. It is this most recent phase of work, conducted primarily by the National Park Service, that has given us a totally new appreciation for just how unusual this area was. In this special volume in the School of American Research *Exploration* series, you will be treated to the latest hypotheses and conclusions about Chaco Canyon archaeology, presented by some of the scholars most closely associated with the research.

The singular culture of Chaco Canyon at its peak in about A.D. 1100 is a striking anomaly in what was otherwise a rather slow, steady development in the prehistoric Southwest. With the increasing importance of agriculture that began in about A.D. 250, the life of people residing in what is now Arizona, New Mexico, and adjacent areas gradually improved, as reflected in the appearance of more productive varieties of domesticated plants, increasingly large settlements, and growing sedentary populations. This progress could be represented on a graph as an undramatic, steadily ascending line, but to depict on the graph what happened at Chaco would require an arresting, if momentary, blip. A dramatic increase in population size and cultural complexity was achieved within a few generations, only to fail in less than two hundred years.

But although the flowering was short-lived, the monumental architecture at Chaco Canyon and the outlying settlements connected to it by road represent the first social, political, and economic experiments in the American Southwest that went beyond the level of the independent village. In about A.D. 900, some spark lit a fire of change in the Chacoan people, and the canyon became a focal point of interacting communities, all probably paying tribute or homage to the inhabitants of Chaco's greathouses.

First leaps toward greater complexity are found throughout human prehistory. In Middle America, they are best illustrated by the Olmec sites that later led to the great civilizations both of the Maya and of the Valley of Mexico. The Chavin society of Peru was the foundation of the important Andean cultures, and similar revolutionary experiments have been recorded wherever civilization subsequently arose. While these efforts at increasing complexity were not always immediately successful—and indeed, many false starts may have occurred—eventually one did prevail. From that point on, the melding of autonomous villages into small chiefdoms, then larger states, and finally empires was inevitable.

For Chaco, the entire experiment lasted less than three hundred years. Later, at Casas Grandes in northern Mexico, the movement toward regional centralization was repeated, but it too failed. When the Spaniards arrived in the Southwest, they were entering a region that had twice pushed toward more complex levels of cultural development. If cultural evolution had been permitted to run its course in the Southwest, what would have occurred? Could the area have supported a complex of small states on the Near Eastern model? Though we can only speculate on this point, it seems highly probable that a more organized, centralized culture would have emerged in time.

When you read this volume, or when you next visit Chaco Canyon, think beyond the magnificent ruins, the compelling architecture, the striking scenery, and the beautiful artwork. Think too of the experiment in political and economic development that took place there, an experiment suggesting that the peoples of the ancient Southwest may well have been on a trajectory of cultural development not unlike that taken by earlier people in other parts of the world. While we marvel at the enormous variety in human cultures, what occurred in Chaco Canyon should remind us how often the themes of cultural evolution are repeated.

DOUGLAS W. SCHWARTZ
School of American Research

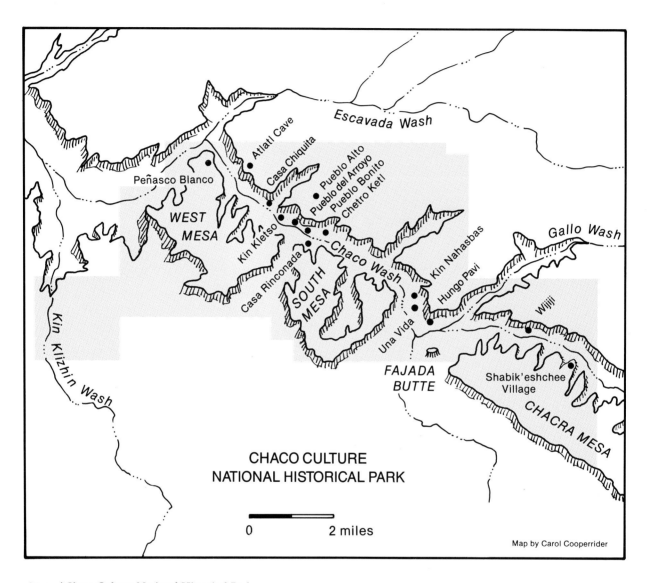

Map of Chaco Culture National Historical Park.

New Light on Chaco Canyon

W. James Judge

WITHIN ITS thirty-two square miles, Chaco Canyon contains more than twenty-four hundred archaeological sites. These range from small scatters of sherds and stone to monumental structures, the thirteen "towns" and the great kivas that the canyon is well known for. Archaeologists have long recognized that Chaco represents a complex culture, but after almost a hundred years of work, many questions about this intriguing phenomenon remain unanswered. We are still not sure how such a sophisticated culture arose in this desolate region, what it was like, or why it collapsed.

Some remarkable findings at the sites have heightened the enigma of Chaco Canyon. First, the number of residential rooms there suggests a population far larger than that which could have been supported by the amount of arable land available. And despite its apparently large number of inhabitants, relatively few human burials have been found in the area. Moreover, a trash

Aerial view of Chaco Canyon from the south, with Fajada Butte in the foreground. Photo by Paul Logsdon, 1982.

mound at one pueblo contains an estimated one hundred fifty thousand broken ceramic vessels, representing 125 per family per year—hardly a plausible rate of consumption under ordinary circumstances. Finally, there are the roads. Though there would seem to be no need for them in a desert area, more than four hundred miles of long, wide roads run out from the canyon in straight lines with little regard for topography.

How do we make sense of these perplexing discoveries? Can what we know about Chaco's development shed light on them? These are questions that I will address in the following pages. A summary history of the canyon will help to clarify how some of the unusual features of its culture may have arisen.

CHACO'S EARLIEST PEOPLE

We know from projectile points found in the canyon that it was occupied some ten thousand years ago by Paleo-Indians. Probably few in number, these mobile hunters subsisted on now-extinct large mammals such as the *Bison antiquus*, which frequented the plains surrounding Chaco. These earliest groups were followed by Archaic peoples, who foraged primarily on small mammals and wild plants. Since their movements were governed by the seasonality of these food sources, their sites were largely ephemeral. Today they are manifest mostly by small scatters of lithic materials such as points, scrapers, knives, and other tools, and by fire-cracked hearth rocks on the tops of the mesas bordering the canyon. Rock shelters offer excellent evidence of Archaic occupation, since deposits in them are protected from the elements. Atlatl Cave, a shelter in Chaco Canyon whose

Atlatl Cave. Photo by David Noble, 1984.

name derives from a piece of wooden spear-thrower three to four thousand years old that was found there, has provided us with extremely valuable information. Perishable materials preserved in the cave include basketry fragments, sandals, spears and spear-throwers, matting, cordage, and vegetal materials such as seeds and seed pods. Primarily as a result of our work there, we now know that there has been no major climatic change in the area for the past four thousand years. There have, however, been periods of reduced precipitation, and as we shall see, these affected farming cultures in the twelfth century, when Chacoan culture had reached its height.

EARLY SEDENTARY OCCUPANTS

Two to three thousand years ago, early farmers began to frequent the Chaco area. They have been termed Basketmaker II after the distinctive woven baskets and sandals they left in caves and shelters throughout the Colorado Plateau; at Chaco they are known from evidence found at Atlatl Cave and a few other sites. The Basketmaker II people were semisedentary hunters/gatherers who may have begun to cultivate squash and particularly corn as early as 1000 B.C. Since these crops do not grow wild, the presence of their seeds and of corncobs indicates agriculture, as do farming implements found in Basketmaker sites. Although these people relied considerably on their corn crops, the return was not sufficient to permit a fully sedentary way of life.

This situation changed beginning in about A.D. 490 with the development of locally adapted strains of corn and probably also with increased precipitation in the Chaco area. Shabik'eshchee Village, in the canyon, was one of the first recognized sites from this early sedentary farming period, Basketmaker III. The dwellings of this time were built in the form of shallow, earth-walled pits roofed with wood and mud-plaster canopies. Small stone rooms behind each pithouse served as storage for food—corn, beans, squash, and a variety of wild plants and animals. A number of Basketmaker III village sites are found in the canyon, some having as many as twenty pithouses clustered close to each other. However, the area's population was still quite small—perhaps one thousand at most—but it was on the increase.

Between approximately A.D. 700 and 900, a basic architectural change occurred at Chaco and throughout the Colorado Plateau. The descendants of the Basketmakers, the prehistoric Pueblo Indians known as Anasazis, made the transition to surface dwellings. These stone masonry structures, which became highly refined during the Classic period at Chaco, were enlarged versions of the Basketmakers' storage rooms. They were built to the northwest of the pithouses, perhaps so as to face southeast, thus taking advantage of the heat provided by the winter sun. The clusters of rooms, or pueblos, were shaped into small arcs.

Basketmaker sandals woven from yucca and other fibers. Courtesy School of American Research collections in the Museum of New Mexico.

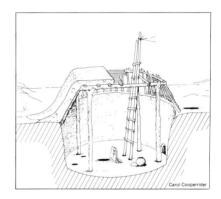

A reconstruction of the architecture of a Basketmaker pithouse.

A pithouse in Chaco Canyon excavated in 1973. Photo by Marsha Truell Newren, courtesy National Park Service, Chaco Center.

This was presumably done so that the rooms would be equidistant from the circular pithouses. The traditional pit dwellings gradually became focal points of ceremonial life and developed into kivas.

During this transitional phase, the residents of Chaco Canyon lived no differently from their neighbors elsewhere in the San Juan Basin and Colorado Plateau. The canyon's population was still only about one thousand to fifteen hundred people in all. But within decades after the beginning of the tenth century, the area experienced major changes—the inception of the unprecedented and sometimes puzzling cultural developments that typify the "Chaco Phenomenon."

THE CLASSIC PERIOD

During the A.D. 900s, Chaco Canyon emerged as the socially most important part of the San Juan Basin. A key to understanding the canyon's role may be the fact that at this time the basin's climate, as recorded in the growth rings of trees, was quite variable. Both quantities of precipitation and its specific location were highly inconsistent; the high-intensity summer rains for which the Southwest is noted were especially patchy.

Three sites located at the confluences of major drainages with the Chaco Wash—Peñasco Blanco, Pueblo Bonito, and Una

The unexcavated ruins of Peñasco Blanco overlook the mouth of a tributary to Chaco Wash. Photo by Paul Logsdon, 1982.

Vida— were apparently the primary scenes of the architectural changes that began in the tenth century. While their general layout of curving surface structures with plazas and kivas immediately to their southeast was virtually the same as that of earlier sites, the buildings themselves were much larger than before, and some units were multistoried. The three sites may have served primarily as storage areas for foods, including both cultivated and wild plants and game such as rabbits, rodents, and antelope, derived from the drainage systems on which they were located. These and other resources could have been pooled at the sites and later redistributed as needed. Such a system would have helped compensate for the inequalities in yields among various areas that would have been caused by the patchy moisture patterns of the time.

These developments in Chaco may have stimulated similar changes elsewhere in the San Juan Basin, primarily its southern half, during the tenth century. Again, their purpose would have been to offset the differences in precipitation that would have created increasing problems as the growing population placed greater demands on limited resource areas. However, as yet there was probably no such thing as a Chacoan "system," and Chaco was not yet in the role of a "central place" in the basin.

One development in Chaco at this time could have provided the basis for the socioeconomic system that emerged later: namely, the canyon's increasingly dominant role in the processing of turquoise into finished articles. Though turquoise does not occur naturally there, Chaco may well have controlled or at least had access to certain sources of the mineral, such as those at Cerrillos, about one hundred miles to the east, near Santa Fe. At any rate, turquoise in various stages of manufacture is found in large quantities in Chaco, and recent work has demonstrated the presence of a number of turquoise workshops among the small villages there. All together, more than sixty thousand pieces of turquoise have been found in the canyon, including heishi beads, pendants, mosaics, and inlays into jet.

We believe that turquoise was initially fashioned into objects of primary ritual importance, but since little has been discovered about the nature of the Anasazi religion, we do not know how these artifacts were used. As an outgrowth of its role in ritual, turquoise may have become more firmly integrated by A.D. 1000 into existing exchange networks that involved both perishable and durable goods. By this time Chaco had become the basin's dominant source of finished turquoise, and it must have been the object of a brisk trade between the canyon and other communities in the southern San Juan Basin. With the growing importance of turquoise, Chaco's role as a ritual center— similar perhaps to that of the lowland Mayan centers in the Yucatan—may also have become increasingly significant. Since poor climatic conditions continued into the early eleventh century, the canyon would have had to rely on both its ritual role and the turquoise trade to offset food shortages.

Three containers full of turquoise beads excavated from Pueblo Bonito by the Hyde Expedition, 1896. Courtesy American Museum of Natural History.

Bird-shaped turquoise beads from Pueblo Bonito. Courtesy American Museum of Natural History.

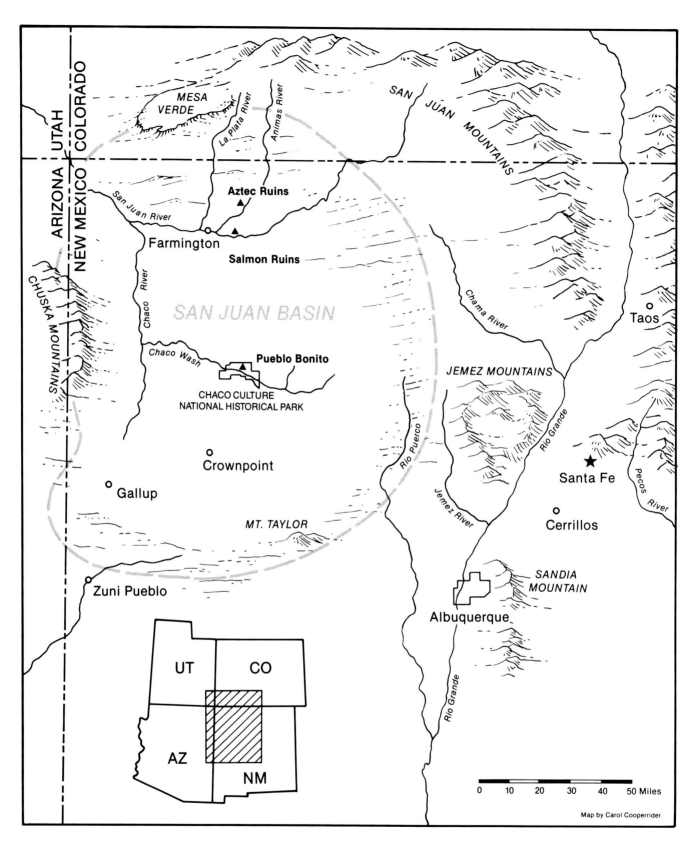

Map of the San Juan Basin and surrounding areas.

View from a tower kiva at Chetro Ketl, one of the largest ruins in Chaco Canyon. Courtesy Museum of New Mexico.

New construction in Chaco may also betoken its growing ritual significance. We know from tree-ring samples taken from preserved beams that work began at this time on Chetro Ketl and Pueblo Alto, both in the central part of the canyon. This investment most certainly indicates that this specific area was becoming important. And since these sites did not control major drainages, factors other than the pooling and redistribution of subsistence goods must have been involved—which again reinforces the idea of a ritual meaning for the area.

Sojourns to Chaco from outlying communities for the purpose of obtaining turquoise would probably have become more formalized during this period, perhaps gradually developing some sort of ritual metaphor that served to "guarantee" adequate rainfall for successful crops. Although we have no direct evidence for such a metaphor, it is implausible that the environmentally marginal San Juan Basin could have sustained a ritual system that lacked some substantive economic basis. Similarly, alliance networks, the systems of trading partners that governed the exchange process, would have become formalized as a means of integrating the communities in the basin. Particularly if turquoise was an important material symbol of the ritual and was controlled by Chacoans, administration and regulation of such exchange networks could well have been the prerogative of canyon residents, some of whom may have attained increased social stature as a result of these developments.

Chuska Black-on-white bowl. Collections of the National Park Service; photo by Deborah Flynn.

THE CHACOAN SYSTEM

In all probability, this configuration of social, ritual, and economic factors was operating as a true system by A.D. 1050; that is, it consisted of a number of interacting but geographically separate communities that were dependent on each other through the exchange of goods and services. The dendroclimatological record indicates that for the next eighty years the San Juan Basin experienced generally favorable weather conditions, which probably supported the continuation of the Chacoan system.

Ceramic vessels discovered in a deep trash mound at Pueblo Alto lend credence to the possibility that a redistribution ritual of some kind took place there. Most of these vessels were imported, chiefly from the Chuska area forty-five miles to the west, but instead of being traded away they were used at the site. The fascinating aspect of this find is that a huge quantity of ceramics was broken: the consumption rate has been calculated at 125 vessels per family per year at Pueblo Alto, compared to an average of 17 at the small villages. The implication is that the breakage was deliberate, but we cannot at this time be certain.

The same Pueblo Alto trash mound also yielded unexpectedly large numbers of animal remains, suggesting that feasts may regularly have taken place nearby. Furthermore, nonlocal lithics, the most common of which are flakes of Washington Pass chert from the Chuska Mountains, were transported to Chaco during the Classic period and discarded unused in the Pueblo Alto midden. Thus several lines of evidence tend to support the idea that ritual consumption of food and imported materials occurred regularly at Chaco Canyon.

This hypothesis might offer an explanation of two other archaeological findings that have stymied researchers for some time. One is the canyon's dearth of burials, which, though they are present, do not occur as frequently here as elsewhere in the Southwest. The determination that Chaco was primarily a ritual rather than a residential area would account for this paucity of human remains.

The other puzzling discovery concerns population. Archaeologists' estimates of the number of people living in Chaco at its peak, based on a count of residential rooms in the towns and villages, range from two to ten thousand; one of the most recent suggested a total of fifty-six hundred. A problem arises here, since reconstructions of the amount of available arable land in the canyon indicate that agriculture there could have yielded sufficient food for at most two thousand people. If, however, the residences were constructed to accommodate periodic influxes of large numbers of people, rather than to serve as housing on a year-round basis, the phenomenon becomes comprehensible. Such influxes, perhaps in the form of pilgrimages from outlying areas, would conform to the hypothesis that the canyon served mainly as a ritual locus.

If this was the case, what was Chaco's constituency? Architec-

Chimney Rock Pueblo, a Chacoan outlier in southwestern Colorado. Photo by Marsha Truell Newren, 1971, courtesy National Park Service, Chaco Center.

tural evidence suggests an answer to this question. During the peak building period in the canyon, from about 1075 to 1115, many outlying communities saw the construction of buildings exhibiting the basic architectural characteristics of contemporaneous canyon structures. By A.D. 1115, as many as seventy communities, dispersed throughout the entire 25,000-square-mile basin, may have been integrated by the socioeconomic and ritual network centered in Chaco. Whether those in control were elites enjoying privileges denied to others, as in similar systems found elsewhere in the world, or were simply members of a dominant social unit remains unclear, but control would undoubtedly have had to be vested in a limited number of people in order for a system incorporating most of present-day northwestern New Mexico and parts of southern Colorado to be administered, maintained, and regulated.

One other important aspect of the Chacoan system becomes more understandable in the context of the ritual pilgrimage hypothesis: namely, the road network that connected many outlying areas to the canyon. Since the Anasazis lacked both draft animals and wheeled vehicles, the roads would appear unnecessary. They can logically be explained, though, as conduits for formal pilgrimages.

How would a system like that suggested above have developed and functioned? It has been proposed that elsewhere in the New World, for example in the Mayan lowlands, pilgrimage fairs or festivals were the mechanism whereby dispersed communities were integrated. Possibly early visits to Chaco Canyon from other parts of the San Juan Basin for the purpose of procuring finished turquoise objects later developed into formally scheduled ritual events or pilgrimages. In conjunction with these,

Ponderosa pine beams, like this one in a roof at Pueblo del Arroyo, were transported to Chaco Canyon from at least thirty miles away. Courtesy National Park Service, Chaco Center.

This bedrock roadway on a cliff above Chetro Ketl was only a small part of the extensive Chacoan road network. Note the border of stones on the right. Photo by R. Gwinn Vivian.

material goods may have been transported along the road system from outlying areas to the canyon and consumed or ritually offered there as part of a ceremony.

One function of the festivals would have been to serve as a forum in which leaders from the various outliers administered the alliances that regulated the exchange of basic foodstuffs and such other essentials as wood, fibers, and lithics. This redistribution would have served to help compensate for any variability occurring in crop production, so that the primary benefit of participation in the network would have been the hedge it provided a community against falling victim to the unpredictable climate. A further advantage would have been the link with a common religious system that, as long as the precipitation regime was favorable, was no doubt perceived as generally successful in providing adequate moisture for agriculture.

Participation in the network must have entailed obligations. These probably included some sort of periodic visits to Chaco and the contribution of goods and services to help maintain and expand the system. Labor would have been important in this regard, since a great deal of manpower was required for the construction of large sites and roads for the transportation of some two hundred thousand beams that were imported into the canyon for use in building.

The Chacoan system evidently functioned quite well as a mechanism for formally integrating a large number of communities in a rather precarious, semiarid environment. The exchange net-

work it provided permitted the survival of a larger population than the area could normally have supported. Considering that the Anasazis had a relatively simple agrarian technology, this is a remarkable achievement. The San Juan Basin was more densely populated during the Classic period than were other parts of the Colorado Plateau or the Rio Grande Valley, and it apparently attracted groups of people from elsewhere in the Southwest, since on the basis of site frequency we know that it must have grown much more rapidly after A.D. 900 than can be accounted for by birth and death rates alone. By the middle of the twelfth century, the basin's population may have been approaching the maximum the system could support—but as we shall see, this may be a moot point.

THE COLLAPSE

By the 1130s, a period of reduced precipitation unparallelled in the previous three to four centuries hit the San Juan Basin. Reconstruction of the climate through tree-ring analysis indicates that moisture was consistently well below average from A.D. 1130 to 1180, and that there were extended periods of consecutive dry years. Besides affecting cultivated crops, drought would have reduced the amounts of wild plant and animal foods available, due to a decrease in total biomass. In a region that was marginal to begin with, a drastic drop in rainfall simply would not allow the continuation of an economic and ritual system already perhaps pushed to the limits of its effectiveness by increased population and maximal interdependence. We have no evidence of construction in the canyon after A.D. 1132, and the area seems to have been virtually abandoned from about 1150 until the next century, when a relatively brief reoccupation occurred. Sites and artifacts from this time found in Chaco indicate that its last inhabitants came from Mesa Verde.

We interpret the depopulation of the canyon and of other places in the San Juan Basin as signalling the collapse of the Chacoan system, but there is virtually no evidence that the ending was particularly traumatic. People seem to have left the region in an unhurried manner, taking their belongings with them. Most probably went elsewhere, perhaps to areas with which they had maintained social and economic alliances, and formed independent communities separate from a large network. Some may have remained in the more environmentally favorable areas of the basin, while others perhaps adopted a mobile way of life resembling that of their Archaic predecessors.

Assuming that a religious ritual was the overt rationale for the Chacoan system at its peak, it too would have been modified, though we have few clues as to how. Possibly the reorganized society that resulted from all these changes was rather similar to modern Pueblo culture, or at least to that culture as it was at the time of Spanish contact.

A CHACO CANYON CHRONOLOGY

B.C.

8500 Paleo-Indians hunting big game in region.

4000 Archaic hunters and gatherers living in region.

1000 Nomadic Basketmaker II people in Chaco Canyon area growing domesticated crops.

A.D.

500 First sedentary population in canyon. Basketmaker III people living in pithouse communities such as Shabik'eshchee Village.

700 Anasazi people living in combinations of pithouses and small, above-ground pueblos.

900 Initial construction at Pueblo Bonito, Peñasco Blanco, and Una Vida, with continued use of pithouses to late 900s. Population growth. Turquoise and pottery trade.

1030 Construction boom and population increase. Building begun on Pueblo del Arroyo and Pueblo Alto.

1100 Chaco system reaches its
1130 peak.

1140 Collapse of regional outlier system. Partial or complete abandonment of outlier and
1175 canyon sites.

1200 Continued population decline, with temporary, limited repopulation by people having
1300 Mesa Verde cultural traits.

1720 First evidence of Navajos living at Chaco.

1823 Vizcarra's Navajo campaign passes through Chaco Canyon—the first recorded European visit.

1863 Navajos removed to Fort Sumner by United States military under Kit Carson.

1868 Navajos return to their homelands.

1896 Wetherill homestead established at Pueblo Bonito.

1907 Chaco Canyon becomes a national monument.

The Chacoan system had risen quite rapidly, yet had evidently been very effective in coping with the harsh environment of the San Juan Basin for almost a century. Indeed, the system was successful enough not only to support the initial population, but also to attract substantial numbers of people to the region while it was in effect. Given the marginal environment, this was no small accomplishment.

Chaco's role as the ritual-cum-administrative center of the basin would have been firm as long as the climate remained generally favorable. As the system expanded, however, it probably became increasingly vulnerable. The very characteristics that gave rise to the Chacoan system's success may paradoxically also have contributed to its downfall, for the network most likely became so large and tightly knit that it could not withstand the extensive environmental deterioration of the twelfth century. The component parts of any true system become more interdependent as its size and complexity grow, so that any single unit becomes more susceptible with the failure of any other. So it may have been with the Chaco Phenomenon.

W. James Judge is chief of the Division of Cultural Research (Chaco Center) of the National Park Service and associate professor of anthropology at the University of New Mexico. He has written many articles on southwestern archaeology, and is coauthor of *Archaeological Survey of Chaco Canyon*.

Chacoan Art and the Chaco Phenomenon

J. J. Brody

Artifacts from Pueblo Bonito, all excavated by the Hyde Expedition in 1896–1899 and now in the American Museum of Natural History. Left: reconstruction of a turquoise-encrusted cylinder; center: deer bone spatula inlaid with jet and turquoise; right: McElmo Black-on-white pitcher. Photo by Deborah Flynn.

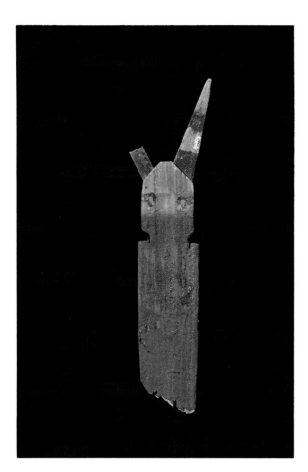

A McElmo Black-on-white pottery canteen from Chetro Ketl. Collections of the Museum of New Mexico; photo by Deborah Flynn.

Fragment of a painted wooden ritual object from a large cache found at Chetro Ketl. Collections of the National Park Service; photo by Deborah Flynn.

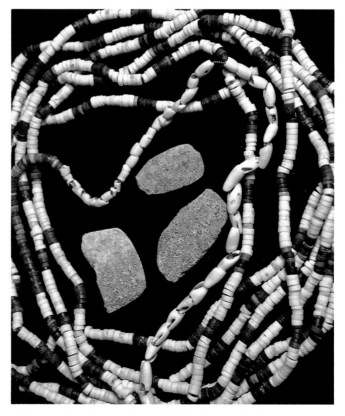

A Chaco Corrugated jar, fifteen inches high. Collections of the Museum of New Mexico; photo by Deborah Flynn.

A fourteen-foot-long necklace of shell and stone beads, along with three pieces of turquoise, all from a wall niche in Chetro Ketl's great kiva. Collections of the Museum of New Mexico; photo by Deborah Flynn.

Human head from an effigy pottery vessel from Pueblo Bonito. Collections of the American Museum of Natural History; photo by Deborah Flynn.

Kiva wall murals incised in plaster at Tseh So, or site Bc50, east of Casa Rinconada. Photo by Paul Reiter, courtesy Maxwell Museum of Anthropology.

THE PEOPLE of Chaco Canyon counted not only architecture but many other forms of art among their achievements. They painted and carved on the canyon's walls, and sometimes they decorated the walls of rooms and kivas with paintings as well. They left behind pieces of painted wood along with small sculptures in wood, stone, and clay, and ornaments of shell, turquoise, and other rare materials. Many of their utilitarian items can be called art too, especially the basketry, textiles, and painted pottery.

What can these arts tell us about a Chaco "phenomenon"? How can they help us better to define the unique qualities of Chacoan life and the relationships between Chacoans and other Anasazis?

In recent years some anthropologists have used the term "Chaco Phenomenon" when referring to the remarkable architecture of Chaco Canyon and to the roads, irrigation systems, and other public works that testify to the apparent complexity of Chacoan culture. By these structures the Chacoans are differentiated from their neighbors. Yet a close look at other Chacoan art forms suggests that the catchy phrase may overstress differences and disguise some fundamental similarities.

Jet frog inlaid with turquoise, recovered from Pueblo Bonito by the Hyde Expedition. Courtesy American Museum of Natural History.

Ceramic cylinder jars from among 114 uncovered by the Hyde Expedition at Pueblo Bonito. Collections of the American Museum of Natural History; photo by Deborah Flynn.

Even the briefest survey of the nonarchitectural arts that survived at Chaco shows them to be more like than unlike those of other Anasazis. The rock art, for example, fits well within Anasazi traditions, and while much of it is distinguished, there are few panels or pictures that are innovative or unusual. Both Chetro Ketl and Pueblo Bonito had sophisticated wall paintings, but their beauty, interest, and originality are comparable to those of murals from several locations in the Mesa Verde and Kayenta regions.

When we compare the marvelous painted, carved, and constructed wooden objects from Chetro Ketl and Pueblo Bonito with quite similar and equally beautiful sculpted forms from Anasazi and Mogollon sites of the same period, it becomes clear that they all belong to a single, pan-southwestern tradition. In like manner, the relatively few surviving baskets and textiles from Chaco are little different from many contemporaneous ones found at other southwestern sites.

Perhaps the most beautiful of the surviving examples of Chacoan art are the carved and inlaid ornaments of shell, jet, turquoise, and bone. Yet these too, when viewed in the larger context of the prehistoric Southwest, must be judged as regional variations of a broadly shared tradition. And the very portabil-

ity of such gems as inlaid bone spatulas and turquoise encrusted baskets allows them to attest only to the wealth and good taste of their Chacoan owners. We do not know what craftsmen fashioned these treasures, or where they lived.

The cylinder vases of Chaco appear to be unique pottery forms, and the fine-line hachuring with which Chacoan potters decorated their wares created color and pattern effects quite unlike those found anywhere else in the Southwest. These differences in pottery style, however, are of no greater order than those that define the Mesa Verde or Kayenta or Chuska pottery painting traditions.

Beautiful things were made at Chaco and used by Chacoan people. But there is a magnitude of difference between the architecture that is the visible, tangible hallmark of what has come to be called the Chaco Phenomenon and the other arts of Chaco. It has been argued that the construction of the greathouses and the great kivas, along with the roads and outliers, provides evidence for levels of social, political, and economic complexity that are more than Anasazi. That argument is not supported by the other expressive arts: except for architecture, Chacoan art was the norm for the Anasazi world.

A Cibola White Ware bowl. Collections of the American Museum of Natural History; photo by Deborah Flynn.

Wooden bird, Chetro Ketl. Collections of the National Park Service; photo by Deborah Flynn.

Stone mortar painted in red, orange, blue, and green, eight and one-half inches high, found by the Hyde Expedition at Pueblo Bonito. Photo by W. Orchard, 1901, courtesy American Museum of Natural History.

A bird of hematite inlaid with turquoise, illustrated in George Pepper's 1920 report on Pueblo Bonito. Courtesy American Museum of Natural History.

How should we interpret this apparent anomaly? How does it affect our understanding of the Chaco Phenomenon?

When all is said and done, the Chacoans were Anasazis. At Chaco Canyon, small, unimposing pueblos were occupied simultaneously with the greathouses, and elsewhere throughout the system, similar communities were associated with Chacoan outliers. Many Chacoans apparently lived in houses little different from those of other Anasazis. In many other respects the Chacoan lifestyle resembled that of other people of the San Juan Basin. Perhaps we should not be surprised to observe that in most of their arts, the Chacoans were again only moderately unlike the other Anasazis.

It may be that the Chaco Phenomenon—whatever it may have been—hardly touched the lives of most Chacoans most of the time. For its own merits, we find it hard to overpraise Chacoan art, but our admiration for it then leads us further to esteem the very similar arts of all the Anasazis.

J. J. Brody is director of the Maxwell Museum of Anthropology of the University of New Mexico. He is an art historian and anthropologist and the author of *Mimbres Painted Pottery*.

Reflections on Chacoan Architecture

William Lumpkins

FROM THE NORTH cliff overlooking Chaco Wash, the magnificent ruins below offer little clue as to how a people, some eight hundred years ago, spent their daily lives. One can only observe the silent stone buildings and conjecture. Seen in the dawn light, the great crescent that is Pueblo Bonito raises questions in the mind of the architect. Who selected the site for this gem of southwestern architecture, positioned above the flood plain, protected from cold north winds by the mesa cliffs, facing the winter sun? How were its rooms, kivas, and plazas used by the people of Chaco Canyon?

The south base line of Pueblo Bonito measures just over five hundred feet. From the center of this line to the apex of the crescent is a distance of 310 feet. The complex is thought to have reached four stories and housed about one thousand people. Truly, Pueblo Bonito was a monumental structure for its own or for any day. How many people built the town? Using the

Pueblo Bonito, the north cliff, and the rubble of the fallen Threatening Rock. Photo by Paul Logsdon, 1982.

One of the four main styles of masonry veneer used as facing for the rubble-core walls at Pueblo Bonito. Photo by David Noble, 1979.

This masonry style dates slightly later than the one in the photograph above. Photo by David Noble, 1979.

A T-shaped doorway at Pueblo Bonito. Photo by David Noble, 1984.

estimated population figure, one can assume a town work force of 250 to 300 people. Not all of them, however, could have been spared at once for construction. Hunting, farming, tool and pottery making, weaving, ceremonies, and other social events and economic tasks would also have demanded time and effort.

In Anglo-American society, construction is traditionally a male job. Early Spanish chroniclers in the Southwest reported that among the Pueblos, women played a large part in building. Was this true in eleventh-century Chaco Canyon? My own belief is that the careful fitting and finishing and chinking evident in Bonito-style stonework reflects a significant input by women.

As an architect, I cannot resist making certain rough calculations, and I conclude that more than one million dressed stones went into Pueblo Bonito's building. This number represents up to one hundred million pounds of stone veneer to be quarried, carried, dressed, and put in place. In addition, there were thousands of ponderosa pines to be felled and trimmed in distant highlands and carried to Chaco Canyon. Many times more ceiling poles were needed—and remember, the Chacoans had no case-hardened tools to shape and smooth their stones and saw their logs. Finally, consider that Pueblo Bonito is only one of more than a dozen major towns in the canyon. How was all this work organized and carried out? The labor calculations overwhelm this twentieth-century architect!

Passive solar heating is a subject of much interest to forward-looking present-day builders. Its principles, however, go back many centuries and can be seen effectively expressed at Pueblo Bonito. The Bonitans designed their apartment building to collect solar heat from the beginning to the end of each winter day. First, the sun strikes the east face of the crescent's west wing, warming the terraces only minutes after breaking over the horizon. Toward midday, the center of the pueblo is warmed, and late in the afternoon, the east wing. How did the people use this advantage in their daily routine? We know from historical observations of Pueblo life that rooftops were ideal and much-used work places. At Bonito, they were sheltered on the north, warmed from the south. In summer, the solar system could have been used in reverse, with workers following shaded areas from the east wing in the morning to the west wing in the afternoon.

Recognizing the beauty and effectiveness of Pueblo Bonito's passive solar design, one wonders why all the Chacoan towns were not planned in similar fashion. Some were, others were not. Perhaps other factors in site selection superseded solar heating. Perhaps some towns were used only in summer. Maybe the planners of towns not utilizing solar heating principles as well as Bonito were simply behind the times. As with many other aspects of Chacoan life, we must seek the answers within our own powers of observation and reason and imagination.

William Lumpkins is a noted architect and artist who has long been inspired by Southwest Indian architectural traditions.

Like Pueblo Bonito, the town of Chetro Ketl, with its back to the north cliff, was well designed for solar heating. Photo by Paul Logsdon, 1982.

A reconstruction of Chetro Ketl by Robert M. Coffin, about 1930. Courtesy School of American Research collections in the Museum of New Mexico.

Pueblo del Arroyo. On the left is its unusual structure with three concentric walls. Photo by Paul Logsdon, 1982.

A decorative touch in a masonry wall at site Bc57, near Casa Rinconada. Photo by Paul Reiter, 1942, courtesy Maxwell Museum of Anthropology.

Five mealing bins with metates and manos, probably from the small pueblo called Bc51, near Casa Rinconada. Photo by Frank McNitt, 1951, courtesy New Mexico State Records Center and Archives.

Above: The outlier site of Peñasco Blanco. Photo by Jim Bradford, 1982.

Left: Sandstone walls at Kin Kletso. Photo by Peggy Wier, 1983.

Below: The unexcavated ruins of Wijiji, possibly one of the last large towns to be constructed in Chaco Canyon. Photo by Paul Logsdon, 1984.

Petroglyph from a room inside the talus unit behind Pueblo Bonito, late 900s or early 1000s. Photo by Jim Bradford, 1979.

The exterior of a tower kiva at Chetro Ketl. Photo by David Noble, 1979.

Overview of Chaco Canyon, facing east. Pueblo del Arroyo is in the foreground, with Pueblo Bonito beyond it. Photo by Paul Logsdon, 1984.

Chaco Canyon Archaeology Through Time

Robert H. Lister

The ruins of Una Vida, with Fajada Butte in the background, drawn by Richard Kern in 1849. Courtesy Library, Academy of Natural Sciences of Philadelphia.

THE LONELY RUINS of Chaco Canyon were apparently first known to Europeans during the mid-seventeenth century. By that time, military parties from Spanish outposts along the upper Rio Grande Valley passed through or within the vicinity of the canyon on forays against the nomadic Navajos. In the following century, a few Spaniards received land grants near Chaco, and a 1774 map seems to identify the canyon's location. Specific references to the ruins were first written by leaders of Spanish military parties in the early 1800s.

A substantial report on Chaco antiquities came with the opening of the American era in the Southwest. Navajo depredations against white settlements were a continuing problem, and American troops replaced Spanish punitive forces. In 1849, a group of soldiers camped in Chaco Canyon for several days.

First Lieutenant James H. Simpson, a member of that party, was so struck by the great array of massive ruins set in such desolate surroundings that he wrote a description of them, documenting seven of the major ruins and several smaller ones.

First Lieutenant James H. Simpson, 1857. Courtesy Minnesota Historical Society.

Photographer William Henry Jackson at Peñasco Blanco, about 1925. Courtesy National Geographic Society.

Names supplied by the Mexican and Indian guides accompanying the party were assigned to the sites. Besides describing some of the ruined towns and their architectural features, Simpson speculated as to who the builders had been, recognized their technical skills, and questioned how they had existed in such a hostile environment. He suggested that the communities might have been founded by peoples who later moved southward to establish the ancient civilizations of Mexico. Drawings and maps prepared by two artist brothers in the detachment, Richard and Edward Kern, supplemented Simpson's 1852 report. However, the obscure account brought little recognition to Chaco Canyon.

As the West was opened for settlement and economic development, various government exploratory and survey parties crisscrossed the region. In 1877, Chaco Canyon was visited by one such unit, the Geological and Geographical Survey of the Territories. William H. Jackson was photographer for that group. Previously, his assignments had taken him over much of the Southwest, where he had examined and photographed many prehistoric ruins and indigenous Indian groups.

Jackson revisited, mapped, and amplified descriptions of the sites previously explored by Simpson. He noted that holes had been poked through the exterior walls of Pueblo Bonito by vandals searching for relics. He also discovered, named, and described three additional large ruins and found the prehistoric stairways in the cliffs behind Pueblo Bonito and Chetro Ketl.

Expecting to be the first to make a photographic record of the intriguing ruins and stark beauty of Chaco Canyon, Jackson hauled his cumbersome eight-by-ten camera around the canyon, making almost four hundred exposures. To his great dismay, when the plates were later processed, they were all blank because of faulty film. Though Jackson subsequently became known as the "Pioneer Photographer of the West," his reputation was not built upon his Chaco work! However, Jackson's 1878 report contained some astute observations. Utilizing his knowledge of other southwestern ruins and of living Pueblo Indians, he correctly identified the Chaco remains as part of a cultural sequence extending from prehistoric times to the modern Pueblos.

During the last quarter of the nineteenth century, the scientific community became interested in Chaco. Victor Mindeleff, of the Bureau of American Ethnology of the Smithsonian Institution, spent six weeks there in the winter of 1888 during part of his monumental study of Pueblo architecture. He had more success with his photographic film than had Jackson, and he produced the first pictorial record of the Chaco ruins.

A smattering of travelers, adventurers, writers, and relic seekers also were drawn to Chaco. Popular accounts of its impressive sites appeared in magazines and books, and some ruins were probed for artifacts.

But despite Chaco's fame, toward the end of the century knowledge of the canyon was still only superficial. Some of the major communities had been discovered, named, mapped, and photographed. However, their ages, architectural details, contents, builders, and role in southwestern prehistory remained shrouded in mystery. Then a series of events led to the first systematic digging in the canyon and ushered in a new era.

COLLECTORS

The world-famous cliff dwellings of Mesa Verde—a mere eighty-five miles northwest of Chaco Canyon—were discovered and explored between 1888 and 1891. From its ranch at the foot of the Mesa Verde, the Wetherill family played a major role in that endeavor, not only finding most of the pueblos in the cliffs but also unearthing large assortments of well-preserved artifacts.

At that time, there developed a widespread interest in the multitude of archaeological remains scattered over the new southwestern frontier. Many individuals, most of them untrained in scientific procedures, dug in the residue of the ancient settlements out of curiosity or for monetary gain. There was a ready market for the artifacts, and no laws prevented their being dug up and sold. However, farsighted citizens saw the value of protecting and preserving the evidences of the past and began to agitate against such destructive activities.

One of the Wetherill brothers, Richard, became so enthralled with searching for the remains of the Anasazis that he spent most of his adult life in their pursuit. He achieved a reputation for finding and digging in many ruins, and for guiding scientists and interested parties to them. From his association with members of the scientific community, he also learned the archaeological methods of the time.

Victor Mindeleff at Chetro Ketl, 1888.
Courtesy Smithsonian Institution.

Copper bell, a trade item from Mexico found at Pueblo Bonito. Illustrated in George Pepper's 1920 report. Courtesy American Museum of Natural History.

Following his work at Mesa Verde and a season in Grand Gulch in southwestern Utah, where he dug under the sponsorship of Talbot and Frederick Hyde, brothers from a wealthy New York family, Richard Wetherill turned his attention to Chaco Canyon. An exploratory trip there in 1895 led him to believe that the canyon's enormous ruins would produce "relics in quantity." He noted that the Chaco ruins were similar to those of Mesa Verde but that they were larger and built in the open rather than in caves. The Hyde brothers agreed to back an excavation program, and the Hyde Exploring Expedition undertook work in Chaco during the summers of the next four years.

The Hydes arranged for Professor F. W. Putnam, of the American Museum of Natural History and Harvard University, to direct the project. His leadership was mainly advisory; he only visited Chaco once during the digging. One of his students, twenty-three-year-old George H. Pepper, was named field supervisor. Richard Wetherill was foreman, and as it turned out, he actually directed most of the fieldwork. Wetherill also assembled and ran the Navajo crew, set up and maintained the camps, and took many of the notes and most of the photographs. The inexperienced Pepper kept some notes, catalogued the items found,

Navajo excavators at Pueblo Bonito during the Hyde Expedition of 1896–1899. Courtesy American Museum of Natural History.

prepared plans of the excavated features, and attended to the administrative records. All specimens were donated to the American Museum of Natural History, where they remain as a valuable study collection. As a sideline, Wetherill established a trading post to cater to the needs of the local Navajos.

The expedition concentrated its efforts on Pueblo Bonito, opening up nearly two hundred of its rooms and kivas. Luckily, Pepper and Wetherill stumbled upon several rooms that had served secondarily as burial chambers. From these, some rather spectacular funerary offerings of pottery and jewelry were recovered. Also, minor digging was done at other sites.

When the research program terminated after the 1899 season, it was roughly estimated that among the items recovered were 10,000 pieces of pottery, 5,000 stone implements, 1,000 bone and wooden objects, 50,000 pieces of turquoise, a small number of copper bells, and a few fabrics. The collection was judged to exceed that from any previous similar effort in this country. In retrospect, it is obvious that the primary result of the expedition was to amass a large collection of specimens. The project cost the Hyde brothers about $25,000.

Pepper's report on Pueblo Bonito, not published until twenty years after the fieldwork, is basically a catalogue of the collection. Emphasis was on objects supposedly associated with ceremonial activities—a common practice at that stage of archaeological interpretation. The report answered a few previously posed questions about Chaco culture, but there was little consideration of the everyday behavior of the Chacoan people.

Pepper noted that artifacts from Pueblo Bonito were similar to those recovered from other ruins in the San Juan drainage. A

At the Wetherill trading post in 1899 are, left to right, T. Mitchell Prudden, George H. Pepper, Clayton Wetherill, Mary Wetherill (Clayton's wife), Richard Wetherill, Jr., Richard Wetherill, and Marietta Palmer Wetherill. Courtesy National Park Service, Chaco Center.

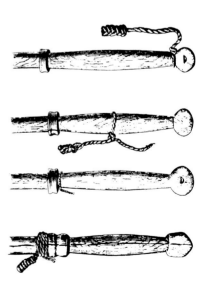

Ceremonial sticks from Pueblo Bonito, as illustrated in George Pepper's excavation report. Courtesy American Museum of Natural History.

lengthy occupation of the canyon was suggested by the findings of superimposed buildings and also by distinctions in architecture, artifacts, and burial practices between small ruins and the
great communal structures. Lacking means of dating his finds,
he could conclude only that the Chaco sites were prehistoric.

The Hyde Expedition planned to continue work at Pueblo
Bonito after the fourth season but was forced to cease excavations because of rising objections to its activities by informed
laypersons and professionals. A similar reaction had manifested
earlier against digging in the Mesa Verde cliff dwellings by the
Wetherills and their associates.

Conservationists eventually prevailed. In 1906, Congress
passed an antiquities act forbidding unauthorized excavation or
collecting of archaeological materials on federally controlled
lands. Mesa Verde became a national park in 1906, and Chaco
Canyon a national monument in 1907; this status assured the
perpetual care of these areas by government agencies.

This phase of Chaco investigation ended with the murder of
Richard Wetherill, who had stayed on in Chaco Canyon as a
rancher and trader to the Navajos following the demise of the
Hyde Expedition. He was shot and killed in 1910, following an
argument with a Navajo. His wife, Marietta, tried to operate the
holdings for several years after his death, but mounting debts
forced her to give them up and move elsewhere. Both Richard
and Marietta are buried in a lonely cemetery within sight of
Pueblo Bonito, the ruin that figured so prominently in their lives.

ARCHAEOLOGISTS, GEOLOGISTS, CHRONOLOGISTS

Following the intense activity of the Hyde Expedition and the
excitement over Richard Wetherill's murder, Chaco Canyon's
characteristic solitude returned. For two decades after the termi-
nation of digging at Pueblo Bonito, little activity took place in
Chaco, although the study of the original inhabitants of the
Southwest was forging ahead elsewhere.

A cadre of archaeologists was doggedly trying to piece together the fundamentals of southwestern prehistory. The concept of stratigraphy was borrowed from geology, permitting better chronological placement of archaeological materials; and the astronomer A. E. Douglass devised a means of accurately dating many ruins, the tree-ring method. The importance of pottery analysis for establishing temporal and cultural relationships was recognized. Archaeologists routinely sought assistance from other disciplines in identifying, dating, and interpreting their data.

Chaco Canyon became a prominent site again in 1921, when the National Geographic Society decided to sponsor a multiyear project to further excavations at Pueblo Bonito and pursue other studies in the canyon. Neil M. Judd, archaeologist at the U.S. National Museum in Washington, was selected to head the program. He was a good choice, for he previously had participated in exploratory and archaeological activities in southeastern Utah and northeastern Arizona.

Judd and his staff of experienced scholars devoted seven summers to the fieldwork. They cleared the remainder of Pueblo Bonito, opened portions of Pueblo del Arroyo, and investigated several pithouses and villages representing the early stages of the Chaco sequence.

The way of life of the long-vanished inhabitants was probed through intensive studies of the architecture, tools, pottery, and other artifacts left behind by the occupants of Pueblo Bonito. The growth and development of the pueblo from a small arc of

Neil Judd and an unidentified companion, 1921. Courtesy National Geographic Society.

Threatening Rock before it toppled onto Pueblo Bonito. Photo by Charles F. Lummis, 1901, courtesy Museum of New Mexico (neg. 6153).

rooms to its final form was documented by examining and mapping architectural details and by the discovery that certain styles of masonry indicated particular spans of time. The latter determination was made possible by tree-ring dating. On the basis of work at Pueblo del Arroyo, Judd believed that an influx of Anasazis from the Mesa Verde region had mingled with the local people during the heyday of Chacoan culture.

The combined efforts of Judd and his coworkers were directed toward other facets of Chaco Canyon prehistory as well. They examined Threatening Rock, the huge sandstone block that stood precariously on a narrow base behind Pueblo Bonito. They also noted evidence suggesting that a network of prehistoric roads had existed in the region. Documenting a succession of cycles of deposition and arroyo cutting in the canyon bottom helped them reconstruct past and recent climatic conditions.

The National Geographic Society's efforts resulted in the development of a postulated sequence for Chaco Canyon culture and also demonstrated the interaction between humans and the austere Chacoan environment. The project identified factors that could have contributed to the abandonment of Chaco Canyon: reduction of farm lands caused by erosion which might have been triggered by the cutting of the ancient pine forest; dwindling food supplies that could have led to internal dissent; and, perhaps, pressure from marauders.

STUDENT ARCHAEOLOGISTS

Edgar L. Hewett waited in the wings for many years before he got his chance to initiate an expedition in Chaco Canyon. A leading opponent of the Hyde Expedition's activities, he had played a major role in bringing them to a halt. His dogged perseverance helped convince political powers of the need for a law protecting antiquities and for placing important archaeological zones under federal protection.

Hewett recognized the importance of the dense concentration of remains from the Anasazi civilization in Chaco and longed to set up an excavation program there, but for years other projects interfered with his plans. Limited research under his direction was begun in 1921, but when the National Geographic Society put its large expedition in the field, Hewett withdrew until that project was concluded.

In 1929, his School of American Research–University of New Mexico investigations were initiated. This effort marked the first time local institutions took a lead in Chaco Canyon archaeology. Hewett, an educator, was associated with anthropology programs at the University of New Mexico and several other academic institutions. He had set up archaeological training programs in various field locations. He and his associates gave students on-the-job instruction in Chaco Canyon for almost two decades, as an integral part of a comprehensive excavation program.

Edgar Lee Hewett at Chaco Canyon. Courtesy Museum of New Mexico (neg. 7374).

Initially, Hewett's School of American Research excavations centered on Chetro Ketl, a ruin slightly smaller than the neighboring Pueblo Bonito. About one-half of the site was eventually cleared. Chetro Ketl became one of the best tree-ring–dated ruins in the Southwest because of an abundance of timbers in its rooms and the presence of many charcoal fragments in its refuse heap. Dates obtained at the site range from A.D. 883 to 1117. The digging of a great kiva in Chetro Ketl and in each of two other isolated sites, Casa Rinconada and Kin Nahasbas, provided information about the engineering and artistic skills of the Chacoan people and insights into their complex religious and social systems.

Later, the archaeological work burgeoned as the popularity of the program grew, and the University of New Mexico built a permanent research station in the canyon to accommodate the hundred students and staff members who annually participated in the field sessions. Attention was turned to a group of small ruins on the south side of the canyon that were thought to have preceded towns such as Pueblo Bonito and Chetro Ketl. Significantly, however, they proved to have been occupied concurrently with the great towns, in a sort of urban-suburban relationship.

The program also involved many projects ancillary to the excavations: reconnaissance of areas in and around Chaco, studies of past climatic conditions, syntheses of data suggesting connections between the Chacoans and contemporaneous Mexican cultures, and studies of the local Navajos.

School of American Research excavation of the great kiva at Chetro Ketl. The Navajo crew is using a winch and mining car on tracks to remove the fill. Courtesy Museum of New Mexico (neg. 66982).

The great kiva of Casa Rinconada, excavated by Hewett, is one of the largest on record, with a diameter of more than sixty-three feet. Photo by Paul Logsdon.

When this stage of Chaco Canyon investigation came to an end, a general outline of the region's prehistory had been established, but many details were still lacking. Some characteristics of the civilization at Chaco were defined, however. Hewett believed that among the traits and tendencies of the Chacoans, the following were significant: predominance of domestic, community spirit; dependence upon agriculture, with hunting as a secondary means of subsistence; resourcefulness in meeting environmental conditions; an exuberant building impulse; mastery of stone masonry; efficiency in ceramic art; and intense religious activity.

PRESERVATION SPECIALISTS

As administrator of the increasingly important antiquities of Chaco Canyon, the National Park Service for years did little to preserve the ruins it was charged with protecting. Judd and Hewett had accomplished some protective measures and restoration at Pueblo Bonito and Chetro Ketl incidental to their excavation programs, but these had not proved very beneficial.

In 1933, the National Park Service selected Gordon Vivian, who had been one of Hewett's archaeologists, to organize and direct a full-fledged stabilization program. Vivian trained a Navajo crew to do the work and constantly sought to develop and improve techniques that would strengthen and preserve walls and other features without damaging their original fabric.

At first, stabilization procedures were directed toward the most extensively excavated sites—Pueblo Bonito, Chetro Ketl, and Pueblo del Arroyo. Next, the work crews attended to walls protruding from unexcavated ruin masses. For several years, enrollees in a Civilian Conservation Corps camp participated in the work. Today, a sizable sum from the Park Service's annual Chaco Canyon budget is devoted to maintaining the stabilized ruins.

There was one notable failure in the Chaco stabilization endeavors: Threatening Rock, a thirty-thousand-ton, wedge-shaped pillar that stood beside the canyon wall to the rear of Pueblo Bonito. Judd had discovered that the pueblo's residents had recognized the rock's threat to their town and constructed platforms beneath it to keep it from falling. In the 1930s, monitoring devices showed that Threatening Rock was teetering ever so slightly. After a series of studies by engineers, measures were taken to arrest the movement. They proved unsuccessful, however, and in January 1941, the stone crashed to the ground, crushing all or portions of sixty-five rooms of the pueblo. Today, visitors have a panoramic view of Pueblo Bonito from a vantage point on the trail built over and around the mass of boulders and rubble that once constituted Threatening Rock.

In more recent decades, the Park Service has salvaged several small ruins eroded by water or impinged upon by construction activities, and has repaired portions of excavated ruins

Gordon Vivian at Chaco Canyon, 1931. Courtesy R. Gwinn Vivian.

damaged by floodwater. Also, part of salvage operations was the clearing of a three-walled complex on the arroyo bank adjacent to Pueblo del Arroyo and the complete digging in 1951 of Kin Kletso. The latter, like several similar communities within the Chaco sphere, was thought by its excavators to be the result of a late intrusion of Anasazis from the north.

In 1957 a visitor center, headquarters building, and several residences for park personnel were constructed in their present location near Fajada Butte. These structures replaced the unsightly buildings that had grown up near Pueblo Bonito. At the same time, remnants of several of the old Hyde Expedition and Wetherill buildings and the University of New Mexico installation were demolished as part of the Park Service dictate to remove all modern structures from the vicinity of the prehistoric remains.

ARCHAEOLOGICAL ANTHROPOLOGISTS AND ECOLOGISTS

After seventy-five years of intermittent investigations, a broad understanding had been reached about the progression of the Chacoan people from their primitive one-room pithouses to their terraced apartment buildings. But many problems posed by the successive teams of archaeologists and stimulated by investigations elsewhere in the Southwest remained unanswered.

Nevertheless, for twenty years following the Hewett era and the excavation of Kin Kletso by the National Park Service, little archaeological research took place in Chaco Canyon. Then in 1971, the Park Service joined forces with the University of New Mexico to establish a multidisciplinary research facility, the Chaco Center, to execute a set of coordinated research projects. The present author, who had been active in southwestern archaeology for over thirty-five years, was named director of the program. Leadership was turned over eight years later to W. James Judge, a former University of New Mexico anthropologist who still heads the investigation.

The first order of business was to make a complete inventory of all archaeological resources within or immediately adjacent to the monument. Surprisingly, this task had never been done thoroughly. Alden C. Hayes, a veteran National Park Service archaeologist, led the survey parties, which recorded and described twenty-two hundred archaeological features in the designated forty-three square miles. Following that, the staff and consultants of the Chaco Center excavated a series of sites representing the entire spectrum of the Chacoan cultural sequence and conducted a wide variety of ecological studies. Careful analyses of the materials and data from those investigations were made by specialists: archaeologists, physical anthropologists, ethnologists, biologists, geologists, ceramicists, chemists, physicists, archaeoastronomers, and remote-sensing technicians. One goal of the research was to show environmental influences on

An archaeologist for the National Park Service digs a test trench with a backhoe—an example of modern excavation techniques. Courtesy National Park Service.

the Chacoans and the means by which the people modified certain elements of their surroundings.

Instrumental in identifying ground phenomena such as roads and water control devices was remote sensing, a complicated analysis of various types of photographs and data obtained from airplanes and other aerial platforms. Ground-penetrating electronic equipment was used to locate subsurface features at some sites and to map ancient garden plots. In the laboratory, computers stored vast amounts of information concerning many types of natural and cultural findings, and selective retrieval of that information facilitated its interpretation. Archaeomagnetic and radiocarbon methods, as well as the long-established tree-ring technique, were used to date individual sites and to establish geological and archaeological chronologies.

Research made clear that at its peak, Chaco culture consisted of a widespread and integrated economic, social, and religious phenomenon encompassing not only the great towns and smaller communities in and near the canyon but also many outlying settlements. This understanding led in 1980 to an adjustment of the boundaries of the monument. The new, larger entity was renamed Chaco Culture National Historical Park. Distant areas that were not part of the old monument are now protected by the boundary extension.

The aims of archaeology and the methods and techniques of accomplishing it have changed greatly since the initial discovery of the antiquities of the American Southwest. The history of the archaeological investigations in Chaco Canyon is not only of interest in itself but is also a dramatic illustration of those changes. It demonstrates how the discipline has grown from the initial stages in which artifacts were collected for the sake of collecting to the current exhaustive theoretical and analytical studies applied to carefully recovered data and materials.

The accompanying articles have drawn upon the century of Chaco Canyon archaeological research. However, by and large they reflect the results of the latest stage of those investigations, when modern technology opened new horizons for understanding Chaco Canyon and its vanished people.

Robert Lister is a senior southwestern archaeologist, and coauthor, with Florence Lister, of *Chaco Canyon: Archaeology and Archaeologists.* Dr. Lister is the former chief of the Division of Cultural Research (Chaco Center) of the National Park Service. His experience in Chaco dates from 1936, when he was a camp boy in a UNM field school there.

The Environment of the Chaco Anasazis

William B. Gillespie

The Chaco Wash during low runoff, with Fajada Butte in the background. Photo by David Noble, 1984.

Typical desert scrub vegetation around Peñasco Blanco. Photo by David Noble, 1982.

AFTER CROSSING miles of dry, inhospitable desert plains, many visitors are surprised to enter Chaco Canyon and see its impressive prehistoric ruins rising above the greasewood and saltbush. A common response is to wonder how the ancient Anasazis could have flourished in an area that apparently lacks the natural resources needed to sustain a large population. A number of questions soon come to mind: Were environmental conditions more favorable in the past? Was there more rainfall and more woodland vegetation? What did Chaco Wash, now entrenched in a deep arroyo, look like when the Anasazis lived and farmed in the canyon? Did some change in these environmental conditions in the A.D. 1100s either cause or hasten the people's departure?

Questions such as these, and the sense of the canyon's inhospitality that inspires them, have also intrigued several generations of Chaco archaeologists. Through the years, numerous interpretations, explanations, or simple speculations have been put forth in efforts to understand the adaptation of the Chaco Anasazis to their environment. Such explanations have necessarily been modified as new information and new methods of analysis have become available. At no time has this search been more active than during the past decade, when studies by geologists, climatologists, pollen analysts, and botanists, as well as by archaeologists, have contributed new, more detailed and varied paleoecological information. Formerly plausible and widely accepted interpretations of past environmental conditions now often appear speculative and questionable. No doubt, interpretations of the past will keep changing as investigations continue.

In the first part of this century, it was widely assumed that climatic conditions *must* have been wetter for Anasazi farmers to have succeeded. As the well-known early-twentieth-century scientist Ellsworth Huntington argued, "Chaco Canyon and the neighboring plateaus today, even with modern methods of irrigation, could support only a fraction of the number of people who appear to have lived there in the past." Huntington reasoned that the location of ruins such as Pueblo Alto on the mesa tops above the canyon indicated that rainfall in the past must have been great enough for the Anasazis to grow corn and other crops.

Today Chaco Canyon receives an average of eight inches of annual precipitation, although this amount varies substantially from year to year. It would need to be 50 percent greater for such mesa-top dry farming to be regularly successful. However, tree-ring and pollen studies from Chaco Canyon and throughout the Southwest indicate that no such dramatic difference in precipitation amounts existed between Anasazi and historic times. While there were undoubtedly periods of above- and below-average rainfall, it appears that long-term average precipitation was not notably different from that of today. Thus, the major farming areas, then as now, were probably limited to the better-watered soils along the valley bottom and the smaller side drainages. It seems unlikely that extensive dry farming in the uplands was ever very important.

While the notion that the Anasazis fared well because of a much wetter climate has not been considered seriously by most archaeologists for many years, a connection may have existed on a smaller and more subtle scale between shifting precipitation values and the fortunes of the Chaco Anasazis. Changes in the pollen production of various plant species and yearly variations in the widths of tree rings from wood remains found in ruins both provide records of prehistoric plant responses to climatic fluctuations. When combined, these two sets of information indicate that the most intensive periods of prehistoric cultural activity occurred when precipitation, especially summer rainfall, was above normal.

A Navajo cornfield in Mockingbird Canyon in the early twentieth century shows that dry farming can be successful in Chaco Canyon's side drainages. Courtesy School of American Research collections in the Museum of New Mexico.

Desert grassland vegetation in Chaco Canyon. Photo by David Noble, 1984.

This graph, part of a larger one prepared by dendroclimatologists William J. Robinson and Martin R. Rose in 1979, shows reconstructed summer rainfall in inches for northwestern New Mexico. The straight horizontal line is the long-term average of 3.1 inches; the lighter line shows annual fluctuations around the mean; and the darker line represents five-year average fluctuations. Courtesy National Park Service, Chaco Center.

Regional pollen studies suggest that much of the northern Southwest experienced slightly higher-than-average precipitation, particularly during the summer months, from about A.D. 950 to the mid-1100s. This time span correlates approximately with population and building peaks in Chaco Canyon. Analysis of tree rings provides evidence of past climatic variation over shorter periods, such as a few decades, or simply year to year. Researchers at the University of Arizona have recently attempted to reconstruct seasonal as well as annual climatic fluctuations. Their results suggest at least a partial correspondence between peaks of construction activity at the large ruins in the canyon and short periods of above-normal summer rainfall.

The tree-ring record shows the start of fifty years of persistently low summer rainfall in about A.D. 1130. This phenomenon coincides with a drastic drop in building activity at the large Chaco sites. At this time, the canyon apparently lost its position as a regional population and economic center. It would be an overstatement to view this extended period of summer drought as *the* cause of the demise of the Chaco Anasazi culture. Still, it may be that this dry period was one of the most important external factors contributing to the destabilization of the regional economic system centered at Chaco and to the partial abandonment of the canyon.

In addition to climate, another aspect of the past environment that has long been of interest is vegetation, particularly woodland vegetation. Most of the canyon and surrounding terrain is presently covered by desert scrub or desert grassland vegetation. The only woodland vegetation consists mainly of scattered juniper trees on the rocky outcrops and denser piñon and juniper at higher elevations. Many archaeologists have believed that this situation was different in prehistoric times. A widely held view has been that when the Anasazis occupied the canyon, there must have been important stands of stately ponderosa pines as

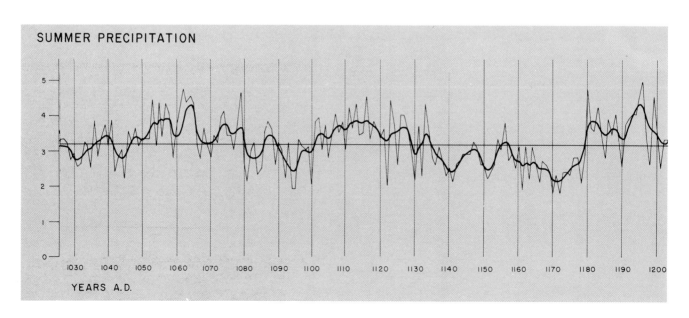

SUMMER PRECIPITATION

YEARS A.D.

well as more extensive woods of the two smaller conifers, piñon and juniper.

One main reason to suspect that ponderosas were locally common is the abundance of ponderosa among the timbers used in construction at the large town sites in the canyon. Wood remains recovered from excavated sites indicate that thousands of mature ponderosas must have been cut for construction of the buildings. In previous decades, researchers reasoned that it is "much more logical" to suppose that the forests were closer than to assume that the Anasazis hauled logs from distant wooded slopes. However, illogical as it may seem, this latter possibility now appears more probable to many archaeologists.

Several lines of reasoning lead to this revised interpretation. Without substantially greater rainfall, it is unlikely that ponderosas could grow in the area except in scattered locations with concentrated soil moisture. More extensive ponderosa woodlands would require much higher precipitation than occurs now, or evidently then either. Studies of pollen, larger plant remains, and animal bones from both archaeological and noncultural deposits fail to document the existence of extensive ponderosa woodlands.

One recent, innovative method for analyzing past vegetation is to examine plant remains embedded in ancient packrat nests or middens. Found in crevices and shelters in the sandstone cliffs, these accumulations include many plants that the packrats collected from the immediate vicinity, and they contain abundant organic materials that can be dated by radiocarbon methods. In Chaco Canyon, researchers from the University of Arizona have analyzed numerous packrat middens, some of which date back eleven thousand years, to a time when conditions were cooler and moister and when trees such as spruce, Douglas fir, and limber pine grew along the cliffs.

Packrat middens from the millenium prior to the Anasazi occupation are abundant and indicate more widespread piñon and juniper woodland than exists at present, but they do not show evidence of a ponderosa woodland. The Anasazis made extensive use of piñon and juniper for building materials and firewood, but they apparently had to go farther afield for most of their larger building timbers.

The pattern of change over time in tree species used in the buildings is also interesting. In the earlier, small Anasazi sites, the majority of identified wood remains are of piñon and juniper. Ponderosa beams became predominant only in the architecturally sophisticated greathouse sites, beginning in the A.D. 900s and culminating in the late 1000s and early 1100s. The increased spans in the large rooms at those sites required longer beams than most piñon or juniper trees can provide. The builders were evidently willing to go out of their way to obtain the needed long, sturdy beams for the imposing multiple-storied structures, whose walls are still standing nine hundred years later. They apparently traveled thirty miles or more south to the Dutton Pla-

Large ponderosa roof support post excavated at Chetro Ketl. Courtesy Museum of New Mexico (neg. 80830).

Navajos crossing the Chaco Wash in flood, about 1930. Photo by Dick Vann, courtesy National Park Service, Chaco Center.

teau near present-day Crownpoint or west to the Chuska Mountains rather than rely on local materials. Other large timbers used in the sites are spruce, Douglas fir, and subalpine fir, species limited to cooler and wetter situations than ponderosa requires and almost certainly not available in Chaco Canyon.

One other noteworthy aspect of Chaco Canyon's past physical environment is the prehistoric appearance of Chaco Wash, the main stream course now confined in a deep arroyo incised in the clays of the valley bottom. For decades, archaeologists have thought that changes in the conditions of this main channel played an integral role in the history of the Chaco Anasazis. Work done in the 1920s led to the traditionally accepted scenario: that the local Anasazi population grew and flourished so long as Chaco Wash floodwaters flowed in a shallow channel that permitted their diversion to fields on the valley bottom. Late in the Anasazi period, it was thought, changing precipitation resulted in entrenchment of the wash into an arroyo. Possibly this development occurred in conjunction with the adverse effects of several hundred years of human impact on the local landscape, which made water in the wash inaccessible for diversion to fields and caused some loss of land. The effects of the arroyo's formation have often been considered disastrous and a main cause of the canyon's abandonment.

Although this reconstruction is widely accepted, there are reasons to suspect its accuracy and applicability. Over the past ten years, detailed examinations of the geological deposits exposed in the valley fill have cast some doubt on the theory's validity. Instead of a single prehistoric arroyo dating from near the end of the Anasazi occupation, there are traces of several entrenched channels. Moreover, it appears that such incised channels existed during at least part of the period of population growth in the canyon, and may even have been the norm. Clear evidence that an arroyo formed near the time of abandonment is lacking. Instead, there are some indications that an arroyo filled in about the time the local population began to wane.

It seems likely that the use of floodwaters from a shallow Chaco Wash for irrigation has been overestimated. Agricultural water-control structures that have been investigated in the canyon are designed to use runoff in small tributary drainages and from the steep slopes of the canyon sides rather than the principal wash. No doubt water in the main drainage was important, but the primary means of obtaining it may have been through shallow wells dug to the subsurface water just below the channel bottom rather than diversion of floodwater during occasions when the wash flowed.

It appears, then, that the importance attached to the presence or absence of an arroyo in the valley bottom has been overemphasized. Although the timing of cut-and-fill episodes in the valley sediments needs to be refined, evidence now suggests that the formation of an arroyo did not have the disastrous effect on the Anasazis that has long been assumed.

In summary, it can be said that the increasing body of information about the past environment is requiring archaeologists to reassess ideas about the adaptation of the Chaco Anasazis. For nearly a century, researchers have thought that the climatic and physical conditions confronting the prehistoric occupants must have differed in some way from the present situation. Undoubtedly they did, but the differences were probably smaller and less drastic than was previously thought. Nevertheless, subtle differences such as occasional periods when summer rainfall tended to be more plentiful and reliable may still have been quite important to the prehistoric residents.

Evidence that conditions a thousand years ago were not greatly different from modern ones makes the Anasazi development in Chaco's apparently marginal environment all the more intriguing. As explanations based on major changes in one or two environmental conditions become more tenuous, archaeologists have begun to consider social and economic variables. Some assumptions and interpretations concerning archaeological remains that have portrayed the development at Chaco as anomalous and surprising are being reconsidered. For instance, the well-preserved, architecturally sophisticated masonry structures may give a false impression of the size and permanence of the prehistoric population. Alternative theories now suggest that far fewer people lived in the canyon than was previously assumed, and that they were more mobile. Most archaeologists have intuitively felt that those expending the effort to build such massive structures must have been permanent, lifelong residents. However, it is possible that some of the people at times moved out to surrounding areas, either on a seasonal basis or for extended periods when conditions were unfavorable in the canyon.

Heavy runoff in the Chaco Wash, like this flood in about 1930, has entrenched the stream into a steep-sided channel. Courtesy New Mexico State Records Center and Archives, McNitt Collection.

Another recent concept presents the possibility that the canyon's population was not dependent solely on local food production. This idea helps resolve the apparent discrepancy between the indications of a large population and the limited potential productivity of farming areas in and near the canyon. It certainly seems probable that the residents of the canyon drew on wild and cultivated resources from a larger surrounding area, though how much larger is debatable. In recent years, it has often been suggested that a wide-ranging exchange network involving outlying communities well away from Chaco Canyon helped support the canyon's population. However, the extent to which food resources were incorporated into this regional economic system remains to be demonstrated.

It seems that the more we find out about the Anasazis and their environment, the more we realize how much we still do not understand. Rather simple explanations of prehistoric events based on the postulate of drastic environmental changes now appear inadequate. Instead, we are beginning to see that the ecological relationships of the Anasazis were undoubtedly quite complex. There is much to learn before we can say we understand what happened in Chaco Canyon.

ACKNOWLEDGEMENTS

The ideas presented here are to a considerable degree based on the recent investigations of a number of researchers, in particular Julio Betancourt, Jeffrey Dean, Steven Hall, David Love, Martin Rose, Thomas Van Devender, and Gwinn Vivian. Each deserves my thanks for contributing—knowingly or unknowingly—to the interpretation given here.

William Gillespie, an archaelogist formerly with the Division of Cultural Research (Chaco Center) of the National Park Service, has written numerous articles and monographs dealing with the archaeology and paleoenvironment of the Southwest.

Outliers and Roads in the Chaco System

Robert P. Powers

Guadalupe Ruin is located on a high, defensible ridge overlooking the Rio Puerco of the East. No prehistoric roads have been identified leading to this relatively small, one-story outlier. Photo by Paul Logsdon, 1982.

DURING THE COURSE of nearly one hundred years of archaeological investigations in the San Juan Basin of northwestern New Mexico, scholars have asked increasingly sophisticated and specific questions. For all our current advances, many basic archaeological questions still are unanswered, although they are now perhaps better defined. The fundamental question remains: Why did the Chaco culture evolve to such complexity in one of the harshest southwestern climates? One hypothesis currently under investigation is that the Chacoans were able to survive and prosper through the establishment of a regulated trade system that equalized the availability of natural resources and agricultural food crops. The purpose here will be to summarize current knowledge about outlying Chacoan settlements, roads, and movement of goods as a basis for examining this hypothesis. The author gives the reader fair warning that many questions cannot yet be answered, and that any journey through the incomplete world of archaeological evidence is as frustrating as it is intriguing. Problems encountered daily by trial lawyers and judges—contradictions in evidence, gaps in information, misleading testimony, and lack of eyewitnesses— are also the fare of archaeologists.

HISTORY OF INVESTIGATION

The Chaco culture was initially thought to occur primarily in Chaco Canyon. Although the canyon's remarkable concentration of large, beautifully constructed pueblos, exemplified by Pueblo Bonito and Chetro Ketl, was immediately recognized as distinct from other known aboriginal remains, most archaeologists in the early decades of this century saw the Chacoans as no more than another interesting Anasazi variant. It was thought that the Chacoan ruins, like the archaeological remains of other Anasazi groups, reflected the culture of a simple, politically egalitarian, sedentary farming people who occupied much of the Colorado Plateau from the time of Christ.

Thus, archaeologists such as Earl Morris, Frank H. H. Roberts, and Paul Martin first viewed the Chacoan architectural styles at the Aztec Ruin, Chimney Rock Pueblo, Lowry Ruin, and Village of the Great Kivas with some puzzlement, since these outlying settlements are as much as 50 or 100 miles or more distant from Chaco Canyon. The significance of these sites was debated for years without general consensus because of inadequate data and because no really convincing explanations were proposed. More recent investigations and the introduction of new archaeological techniques reveal not only that sites with Chacoan features were common and linked by roadways, but also that these comprised the material remains of a surprisingly complex culture. The term "Chacoan outlier" is now commonly used to refer to sites with Chacoan architectural features located outside Chaco Canyon.

CHACOAN OUTLIERS

The outlying Chacoan structures, like their counterparts in the canyon, are massive, well-planned pueblos with distinctive architectural features. These include thick walls of core and veneer, Chaco-style masonry,* large interior rooms, and subterranean kivas with distinctive furnishings. Other, less consistently occurring features of the Chacoan structures, or greathouses, are great kivas, which are large versions of the small kiva; multiple-storied construction; walled plazas; and tower kivas, a rare form several stories in height.

It is apparent that by A.D. 900–975, the period of the first large construction projects in Chaco Canyon, the earliest outliers were being established in the San Juan Basin. During the next hundred years, additional outliers were built at a moderate pace. And in the last quarter of the eleventh century, a large number of sites was constructed in the San Juan River area during a building spree that lasted until A.D. 1140. After this date, no construction is known, and abandonment of some sites may have begun almost immediately. Others were partially occupied until about A.D. 1225, but it is clear that by 1175 the populations of the major Chaco Canyon sites and outliers were much reduced, and that they had ceased to function as members of a coordinated system.

*Chaco-style masonry is distinguished by the use of different shapes and sizes of sandstone blocks, slabs, and spalls mortared with mud in various combinations to create distinctive masonry patterns or styles.

Village of the Great Kivas, a Chacoan outlier in the Nutria Valley near present-day Zuni Pueblo, was excavated by Frank H. H. Roberts, Jr., in 1930. Photo from Bureau of American Ethnology Bulletin III.

The tower kiva at Kin Ya'a, a Chacoan outlier in the Red Mesa Valley south of Chaco Canyon. The prehistoric roadway known as the Great South Road passes through this ruin. Photo by Jim Bradford.

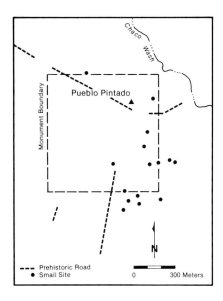

Archaeological surveys allow mapping of the small sites clustered around larger Chacoan outliers, as shown in this map of the Pueblo Pintado community.

Outlying Chacoan structures usually appear amidst a cluster of five to twenty-five pueblos that are relatively small and lack the large-scale planning and careful, skilled craftsmanship evident in the architecture of the canyon proper. It was at these sites that the great majority of the population lived and performed the daily round of secular and religious activities. In addition to the Chacoan structure and a varying number of small houses or pueblos, a great kiva and a road are common, though not ubiquitous, features of such communities.

At least forty outliers are widely distributed throughout the basin, primarily in areas where floodwater or irrigated agriculture could have been practiced. The size and number of sites present at a community probably reflect to a high degree the availability of critical natural resources, such as stone, timber, and water, and the productivity of local arable land. The sites, such as those at the Salmon and Aztec ruins, are usually con-

Salmon Ruin, a major Chacoan outlier on the north bank of the San Juan River, was excavated in the 1970s and today has a visitors' center and museum. Photo by Paul Logsdon, 1982.

structed on valley slopes or ridges near to, yet overlooking, valley-bottom agricultural areas.

Less frequently, outlying Chacoan structures were built on high mesas and promontories overlooking the surrounding community and agricultural lands. Elevated locations may have had signaling or defensive purposes, but if so, these functions either were less critical or were filled in some other way at most of the outliers, which do not share such elevated locations. It is intriguing that Chimney Rock, Twin Angels, Pierre's, Bis sa'ani, and Guadalupe, all situated on high, impregnable mesa tops, are scattered along the apparent eastern frontier of the Chacoan system. The possibility that these sites were so placed for defensive purposes has thus far received little attention or investigation.

We have only incomplete knowledge of the development over time of differences in size among Chacoan structures—including those both at Chaco Canyon and in outlying areas. However, it is clear that by A.D. 1140, distinct differences in the sizes and architectural characteristics of Chacoan structures had emerged. These differences indicate a three-level size hierarchy—large, medium, and small—which may provide important clues to social, political, and perhaps ceremonial differences among the inhabitants of Chacoan structures.

Three of the four largest such structures—their average size is 17,991 square meters or 193,660 square feet—are in Chaco Canyon. The seven medium-sized structures (average size 8,072 square meters or 86,889 square feet) in the next group are, with one exception, also in or near Chaco Canyon. Unlike the large and medium sites, the majority of small Chacoan structures (averaging 1,172 square meters or 12,616 square feet) are at the widely scattered outlier communities. Once all the known Chacoan structures are grouped into these size categories, it becomes apparent that multiple stories, walled plazas, and great kivas occur most consistently at the large and medium sites and become rare as size decreases.

At the pinnacle of the size pyramid are the two largest Chacoan structures, Chetro Ketl and Pueblo Bonito. Each had a large enclosed plaza, up to four stories, and more than five hundred rooms. Their size and central position in Chaco Canyon, at the postulated convergence point of all incoming roads, suggest that these were the most important, powerful centers in the Chacoan system, and that their occupants controlled the entire network of Chaco Canyon and outlying sites. A number of other large and medium-sized sites, such as Peñasco Blanco and Pueblo Alto, are located on natural entry routes to Chaco Canyon, near a major incoming road. Although these sites also had large enclosed plazas, they had only one to three stories and between one hundred and three hundred rooms. Their lesser size and their association with a single major road identifies them as being of intermediate importance. These settlements may have been in direct control of one road system and all of its affiliated communities. At the third and lowest level of the hierarchy of Chacoan

Aztec Ruin, on the Animas River some fifty-five miles north of Chaco Canyon, exemplifies the large Chacoan outliers. The site was excavated by Earl Morris between 1916 and 1920 and today is administered as a national monument. Photo by Paul Logsdon.

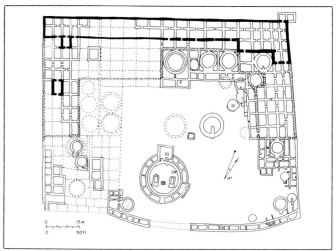

Plan of Aztec Ruin, which had an estimated 405 rooms and 28 kivas. Drawing by Jerry Livingston, courtesy National Park Service, Chaco Center.

A medium-sized outlier, Pueblo Pintado was first recorded in this 1849 painting by Richard Kern. Historian David Brugge believes that Pueblo Pintado was reused in the late 1800s for a trading operation. Courtesy Library, Academy of Natural Sciences of Philadelphia.

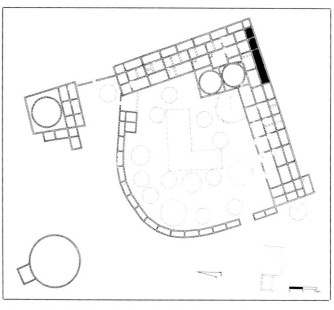

Plan of Pueblo Pintado. Drawing by John Stein, from Anasazi Communities of the San Juan Basin, *Marshall et al., 1979.*

Kin Klizhin, near Chaco Canyon, is a small outlier with a tower kiva. A prehistoric road leads directly to this site. Courtesy Museum of New Mexico (neg. 80700).

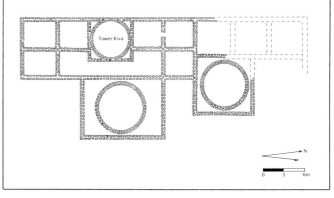

Plan of Kin Klizhin. Drawing by John Stein, from Anasazi Communities of the San Juan Basin, *Marshall et al., 1979.*

structures are the small, widely dispersed outliers, each with its attendant community. The majority of these lacked enclosed plazas, were one to two stories in height, and had less than fifty rooms. Because these small outlying Chacoan structures are typically situated beside the incoming road and are larger than all other buildings within the community, they appear to have been not only the most important edifice in each locale but also the primary entry point and link with other communities.

While most archaeologists agree that all Chacoan structures, regardless of their size, were important community sites, the purpose of the buildings at each of the hierarchical levels and the role their inhabitants played is still unclear. Much uncertainty exists because only a few such structures, and a particularly small number of outliers, have been excavated. As more excavations are conducted, more information will become available—but even careful archaeological excavation does not always provide unequivocal answers. The presence of hearths, corn grinding implements, storage bins, and other household artifacts revealed by excavations at Salmon and Aztec ruins and at Pueblo Alto indicates that portions of these structures were residences, just as were the small pueblos around the Chacoan structures.

The architectural and locational prominence of these buildings in relation to others in the community suggests that they were not just ordinary residences but living quarters for a chiefly or priestly elite, dominant in community affairs. A few burials excavated from Pueblo Bonito by the Hyde Exploring Expedition in the late 1890s have recently been interpreted as the remains of high-status or elite individuals. This theory lends limited support to the idea that a preeminent, controlling group was present at the largest Chaco Canyon sites. Whether such an elite population existed is a controversial question, and much more burial evidence is required before a definitive answer is possible. If a chiefly or priestly elite did develop, it probably did not evolve before the eleventh century. This group was likely small, and elites may have resided only in the large and medium-sized Chacoan structures in the canyon and at the outlying Chacoan structures in large communities.

Some rooms in these buildings are barren and featureless, which raises the possibility that they were utilized for community storage, perhaps of foodstuffs or trade goods. Another alternative is that they were used only on an intermittent or seasonal basis by participants in ceremonial gatherings or pilgrimages. A final possibility is that these empty rooms had no specific purpose other than as locations for displays of the power and, perhaps, the wealth of the elite.

Regardless of their intended use, Chacoan structures in the canyon and at many of the outliers would have required a substantial work force to complete. It is probable that the construction gangs consisted primarily of inhabitants of the smaller masonry pueblos.

In this aerial photograph taken at sunset, three prehistoric roadways can be distinguished converging on Pueblo Alto. A fourth road passes to the left of the site. Photo by Paul Logsdon, 1982.

CHACOAN ROADS

In the last fifteen years, use of aerial photography to identify archaeological features has resulted in the identification of over four hundred miles of prehistoric roadways associated with Chacoan outliers. The Bureau of Land Management and others have recently conducted investigations to delineate the extent of the road system, which was noted and described in the early 1900s by the Wetherills, S. J. Holsinger, and Neil Judd. Additional roads will almost certainly be discovered as investigation continues. At present, as many as thirty outliers can be linked to one or more of six major road systems, each at least 20 miles in length. The longest, best-defined roads extend 40 to 60 miles and connect as many as half a dozen outlying sites to each other and to Chaco Canyon. Because all major roads appear to converge in the canyon, it has been postulated that Chaco was the center of the entire basin-wide network of roads and outlying sites. Although the dates of the roads remain uncertain, most were probably constructed between A.D. 1075 and 1140.

The now-elusive vestiges of the roads, visible on the ground only on certain types of terrain or under specific lighting conditions, are more readily distinguishable in aerial photos, in which they appear as narrow lines of a darker hue than the surrounding landscapes. Physical indications of roads on the ground are slight. In cross section, they are visible as wide (8 to 12 meters or 26 to 39 feet), shallow, concave depressions only a few centimeters deep. Road edges are sometimes demarcated by low berms of broken substrate, rock, and sand excavated during construction or maintenance. Less commonly, masonry curbing, scatters of potsherds, or cuts through a dune or slope testify to the presence of the road. On the roads traversing the cliffs in Chaco Canyon, masonry steps, stairs cut in bedrock, and masonry ramps were used to connect road sections. The generally straight, undeviating bearings of the roads suggest that they were laid out or "engineered" prior to their actual construction, although what specific techniques were used is not certain. Minor realignments in bearing are often detectable on ridges and at other points of minor topographic prominence, a fact that suggests the builders sighted on a distant horizon point but also used intermediate points for short-distance sighting. Corrections in course were made at these intermediate points, where greater elevation allowed the bearing to be rechecked.

Because the Chacoans had no wheeled carts or draft animals, perhaps the most common and stimulating questions concerning the roads are why are they so wide and what were they used for? Unfortunately, no really satisfying answer to either question is possible. We might speculate that the roads were wide to accommodate certain types of ceremonial foot processions or to allow transportation of building materials. However, no material remains supporting either of these possibilities have been recovered from excavations of the roads or the outliers. The fact that major roads appear to connect directly the Chacoan structures in outlying communities with those in Chaco Canyon suggests that the roads' purpose was to facilitate travel and communication between these sites. Yet some shorter roads appear to lead to quarries, possible water sources, and other small archaeological sites. Thus, the question of the exact purposes of the roads—whether for trade, processions, resources, defense, or simply to ease travel—remains open for the present.

The Jackson Staircase, named after the pioneer photographer W. H. Jackson, ascends the north wall of Chaco Canyon near Chetro Ketl. Courtesy Museum of New Mexico (neg. 81733).

Archaeologists examine a low stone wall edging a prehistoric road segment. Photo by Milo McLeod, 1972, courtesy National Park Service, Chaco Center.

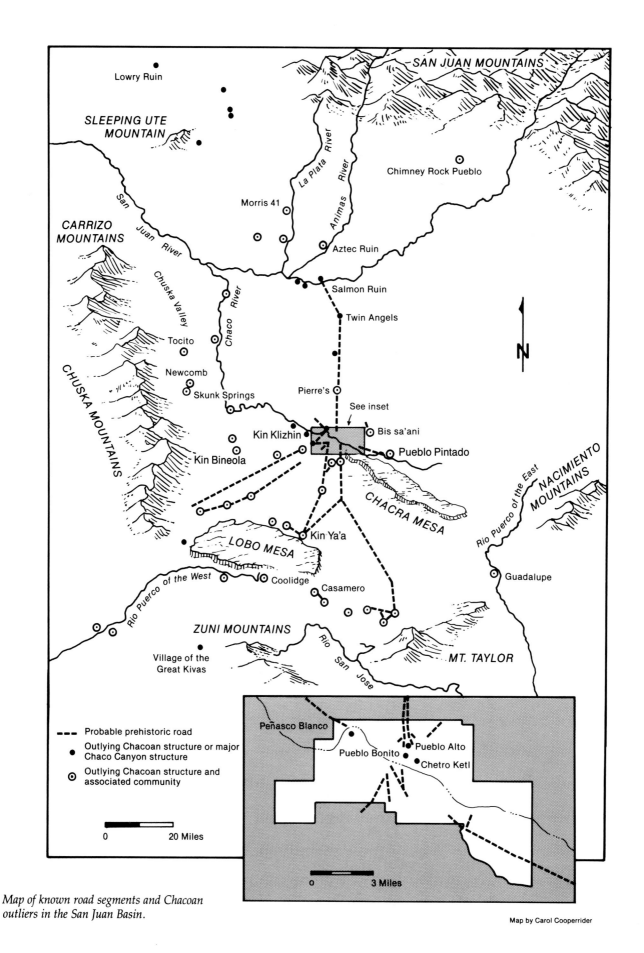

Map of known road segments and Chacoan
outliers in the San Juan Basin.

Map by Carol Cooperrider

INTERACTION BETWEEN THE OUTLIERS AND
CHACO CANYON

Spurred by the realization that roads and outlying sites are elements of an integrated system, archaeologists are conducting research to learn why such a system was developed and what purpose it served. One explanation currently under investigation is that differences in the availability of natural resources among various areas in the system provided stimulus for trade, and that outliers and roads may have been constructed to facilitate and regulate this activity.

Because the San Juan Basin embraces an area of twenty-six thousand square miles that includes landscapes ranging from pine and fir forests to desert shrub or grasslands, is not surprising that the physical and natural environments of outliers vary from location to location. Many communities in the central, lowland portions of the basin, including Chaco Canyon, receive less rainfall than outlier communities situated on the south, west, and north edges of the basin. They also lack permanent streams or rivers and have poor soils and fewer usable natural resources. Intertwined with these factors is a variable that would have been of extreme importance to the agriculturally based Chacoans: unpredictable summer rainfall. Because of the haphazard nature of summer thunderstorms, which may drench one area yet bypass another, crops at an outlier may have prospered one year, only to fail miserably the next.

The cumulative effect of all these differing environmental conditions may have been a need for basin-wide redistribution of natural resources and food crops. Archaeologists hypothesize that such a redistribution system would have enabled residents of an outlier community to receive foodstuffs or goods from a central place where these trade items, collected from other communities, had been stored for reapportionment. It has been proposed that Chaco Canyon, with its large structures and its apparently central position in the road system, was the heart of this reallocation network. Theoretically at least, crops would fail in only a limited number of areas during each year, so those communities experiencing crop failure could be subsidized by surpluses from other communities. Such loans might be repaid in craft products, raw resources, labor, or a surplus of agricultural products in a subsequent year.

The hypothetical nature of this interpretation is emphasized here because as yet only limited archaeological data have been found to support it. For example, no detailed study has focused on the existence of a real need for food redistribution, nor on the ability of communities to produce surpluses. Good evidence for trade and redistribution of other resources is limited, although two types of goods—pottery and stone chipping materials—have been the subjects of in-depth studies. Only the evidence for ceramic trade will be discussed here because stone exchange was low in volume, and in any case this material displays some of

Potsherds from the kinds of ceramic vessels that were traded into Chaco Canyon. Photos by Deborah Flynn.

Left: Red Mesa Black-on-white from the Red Mesa Valley; right: Tohatchi Neckbanded from south of Chaco Canyon.

Left: Nava Black-on-white; right: Blue Shale Corrugated; both from the Chuska Valley.

Left: McElmo Black-on-white from the San Juan River Valley; right: Wingate Black-on-red from west of Chaco Canyon.

the same trade patterns as those observed for ceramics.

Current knowledge of the ceramics trade is incomplete because of the general lack of detailed studies of outliers and our inability to determine the sources of many pottery vessels. However, limited information from surface surveys of outliers and detailed information from a few excavations permit a partial, generalized portrayal of this trade. These studies indicate that substantial quantities of ceramics—primarily unpainted gray ware (culinary) vessels—were traded throughout the life of the outlier system. Painted white and red ware vessels were also traded, but in apparently smaller quantities.

These trade ceramics appear to have come from outliers in at least three major areas: the Red Mesa Valley, 43 miles to the south of Chaco Canyon; the Chuska Valley, 37 miles to the west; and the San Juan River Valley, 47 miles to the north. Although specific outliers cannot be identified as sources, it is likely that one or more outlier communities in each area were craft centers for pottery vessel production: perhaps Coolidge and Casamero in the Red Mesa Valley; Skunk Springs, Newcomb, and Tocito in the Chuska Valley; and Salmon, Aztec, and Morris 41 in the San Juan Valley.

It is interesting that the quantities, or in some cases the predominance, of imports from each of the three general source areas appear to shift over time. Imports to Chaco Canyon from the Red Mesa Valley were seemingly frequent during the tenth and early eleventh centuries, as these account for up to 30 percent of all culinary vessels from this time found at selected canyon sites. During the eleventh and early twelfth centuries, Chuskan ceramics are dominant, accounting for up to 60 percent of the culinary pottery of this period at selected sites. San Juan Valley area white ware ceramics are most frequent at Chaco Canyon sites in the late 1100s and early 1200s, but they never account for more than a minor percentage of all imports. The magnitude of the ceramics trade is indicated by the fact that as many as one hundred fifty thousand separate vessels are estimated to be in the trash mound of Pueblo Alto in Chaco Canyon alone, and that of these, one-third are Chuskan imports.

Ceramic trade data whose accuracy is comparable to those on ceramics from excavated Chaco Canyon sites are not available for most outliers; however, it is known that trade ceramics occur at many sites in the same road systems as the source communities for the pottery. These trade ceramics are also found at nearby outliers in adjacent road systems. It also appears that Chaco Canyon was a major export destination, and that once goods arrived there, they were used rather than redistributed to outliers on road systems distant from the area of production. For example, while Chuskan ceramics occur in substantial quantities throughout the west-central portion of the San Juan Basin and Chaco Canyon, only small numbers of Chuskan ceramics found their way to southern outliers in the Red Mesa Valley or to the Mount Taylor area.

The significance of this trade in relation to the functioning and origin of the outlier system cannot yet be determined with any certainty. On one hand, it seems obvious that the roads and established ties between outliers and the Chaco Canyon sites would have facilitated and perhaps increased trade. Still, it is not at all clear that the original purpose of the system was to promote such economic interaction; there is little evidence to indicate that either critical economic items, such as foodstuffs, or goods of limited availability were exchanged. Thus, it is not known whether this trade was an important purpose of the system or merely a beneficial, and for a time burgeoning, by-product of it.

One of the most interesting findings is that the trade goods studied were consumed in Chaco Canyon rather than being redistributed to other parts of the system. This evidence certainly lends substance to hypotheses that the canyon was a political, economic, and ceremonial center, dominated by a chiefly or priestly elite. However, it does not support the idea that this elite-controlled center gained or attained its position by storing and then redistributing needed goods and resources. Neither does it entirely disqualify the redistribution hypothesis from further consideration; other types of resources not yet investigated may have been redistributed from the canyon.

The available evidence on trade, however limited in scope, does provide a tantalizing view of the functioning of one aspect of the system. It is tempting to stretch this information a bit further and see the changes in outlying sources of trade over time as indicative of system instability. From this perspective, there is a very good possibility that control over the system emanating from Chaco Canyon was quite tenuous, short in duration, and subject to major shifts in alliances with the outlying communities.

Particularly during the tenth century, and perhaps up to the time the road system was constructed in the mid- or late eleventh century, little evidence indicates that Chaco's inhabitants exerted control or influence over outlying areas, even though Chaco quite clearly was a major trade and population center. By the late 1000s, and certainly by the early 1100s, Chaco had probably assumed the more dominant, perhaps dictatorial, role suggested by the appearance of the road system and Chaco's apparent ability to attract trade goods.

Major events during this period include a tremendous build-up of outliers in the San Juan River area, accompanied by the appearance in Chaco of very limited quantities of trade ceramics from that area and a concomitant decrease in Chuskan trade ceramics. Chaco's collapse occurred sometime after A.D. 1140, but probably prior to 1180. The possibility that this development was abetted by strife with the increasingly large and presumably influential populations of the San Juan outliers, such as Salmon and Aztec, should receive future attention.

The collapse of Chaco as the center of the regional system was probably precipitated by the onset in A.D. 1130 of a fifty-year

Chuska Black-on-white bowl. Collections of the Maxwell Museum, photo by Deborah Flynn.

summer drought, which had disastrous consequences for Chacoan farmers in the western and southern San Juan Basin. Even in the best of times, these areas lacked permanent agricultural water sources and so were dependent on scanty summer thundershower runoff for agriculture. It is probable that during many years of this dry interval, no crops were produced in Chaco Canyon or at most outliers. If a food redistribution system was in operation, we may assume that it failed. Only the northern outliers with the capability of tapping mountain snow melt from the San Juan, La Plata, and Animas rivers would have withstood the drought in relative comfort. In such a weakened state, the system could have been mortally damaged by any challenge to the canyon authority or by the northern outliers' refusal to share agricultural crops with Chaco Canyon and the southern outliers.

The aim of this short and much simplified discussion has been to reveal that recent research at both the Chacoan outliers and Chaco Canyon sites is producing new and stimulating ideas and results. The canyon, the outliers, and the interconnecting roads are the remaining evidence of one of the most complex southwestern prehistoric societies. Had the system been able to survive the critical A.D. 1130–1180 drought, it is possible that the prehistory and history of the Southwest would have been quite different.

ACKNOWLEDGMENTS

The data and many of the interpretations presented here are the result of much research by a large number of scholars representing numerous disciplines. Although it is impossible to acknowledge everyone, the following organizations and individuals deserve special recognition: W. James Judge, H. Wolcott Toll, Catherine C. Cameron, Thomas C. Windes, Marcia L. Newren, William B. Gillespie, Nancy J. Akins, John D. Schelberg, and Stephen H. Lekson, all past or present research staff of the Division of Cultural Research, National Park Service; Chris Kincaid, Fred L. Nials, John R. Stein, Margaret S. Obenauf, and Daisy F. Levine, Bureau of Land Management, Chacoan Roads Project; Cynthia Irwin-Williams, Rex K. Adams, Hayward H. Franklin, Philip H. Shelley, and Larry L. Baker, San Juan Valley Archaeological Project; Cory D. Breternitz, David E. Doyel, and Michael P. Marshall, Navajo Nation Cultural Resource Management Program, Bis sa'ani Community Study; and last, but certainly not least, R. Gwinn Vivian, Arizona State Museum.

Robert Powers is an archaeologist with the Division of Cultural Research (Chaco Center) of the National Park Service and coauthor of *The Outlier Survey: A Regional View of Settlement in the San Juan Basin.*

Rock Art in Chaco Canyon

Polly Schaafsma

ROCK PAINTINGS and petroglyphs have been made in Chaco Canyon for at least two thousand years. From the paintings of the Basketmakers in the first five hundred years A.D. to the inscriptions of twentieth-century travelers, rock art reflects the cultures and activities of the people who have lived in or passed through the canyon. Most of the art, however, consists of stylized representational and abstract forms that date from Chaco's long Anasazi occupation.

We do not know whether any art from the Archaic period (ca. 5000 B.C. to A.D. 1) exists in the canyon, but some curvilinear, nonrepresentational petroglyphs may be this early. The first Chacoan art we can date with any certainty consists of Basketmaker II paintings from Atlatl Cave. These plain, triangular-bodied people and myriad handprints are similar to Basketmaker figures found elsewhere in the eastern San Juan region. Con-

Basketmaker figures and a small animal painted in red, Atlatl Cave. Photo by David Noble, 1984.

Painted handprints, probably of Anasazi origin. Photo by David Noble, 1984.

Petroglyph panel consisting largely of pecked Anasazi motifs, including several human figures, rectilinear lizard forms, a mountain sheep, spirals, and geometric designs. Photo by David Noble, 1984.

spicuously absent from this whole area is the distinctive Basketmaker II graphic complex found to the north and west; it typically depicts large and often elaborately decorated anthropomorphs, sometimes accompanied by birds, yucca plants, and, most commonly, handprints. In Chaco as throughout the San Juan area, handprints in such contexts are thought to represent prayers made to establish rapport with supernatural forces.

Later Anasazi rock art in Chaco is characterized by a myriad of figures. The repertoire includes hand-, foot-, and sandal prints; fluteplayers; rectilinear human forms usually depicted as stick figures; animals, including mountain lions and sheep, lizards, and wavy lines that may represent snakes; sheep and/or deer tracks; and two-legged creatures of unknown identity. Spirals are an especially common motif, and there are occasional geometric designs. No developmental sequence for Chacoan Anasazi rock art after A.D. 500 has been established, but the general Anasazi trends probably hold for Chaco. These include a tendency toward increasing rectilinearity and formal geometric patterns, as well as a growing prevalence of spirals and lizards.

The content of the Anasazis' rock art reflects their ideology and values. Fertility themes, often represented in panels with fluteplayers, are particularly evident. For centuries this mythical figure has been associated with the summoning of clouds and moisture, the germination of plants, and the fertility of animals and people. The fluteplayer's role—to help maintain balance in the cosmos—was an essential one in the Anasazi world.

Anasazi rock art in Chaco is found not only in association with habitation sites but also in isolated parts of the canyon away from other archaeological remains. The question of what pur-

pose this graphic imagery may have served has not been addressed. One notable exception is the petroglyphs near the top of Fajada Butte, to which have been ascribed calendrical functions. A large spiral on the butte is situated in such a way that it is bisected by a shaft of sunlight on the summer solstice, and a second, smaller spiral on the same rock face is marked by a ray of light on the equinoxes. Anasazi spirals and other designs elsewhere might have served similarly as calendrical markers, useful in regulating the ceremonial and agricultural cycles of the prehistoric farmers. Studies made outside of Chaco Canyon suggest that Anasazi rock art may have defined social space associated with cliff dwellings, signified social affiliations, or marked shrines and property boundaries.

Most of the historic-period rock art in Chaco Canyon is of Navajo origin. Navajos lived here from the early eighteenth to the mid-twentieth centuries, with a probable hiatus between about 1820 and their return from Fort Sumner after 1868 (see Brugge, this volume). Their rock drawings, which are mostly representational, reflect the cultural changes and experiences embraced by this period.

Lizards became important in Anasazi rock art iconography after about A.D. 1000.

Pecked supernaturals with feathered headdresses in the Navajo Gobernador style, Chacra Mesa. The second figure from the left holds a fox skin. Photo by David Noble, 1984.

Incised Navajo ye'i, probably late 1700s. Photo by David Noble, 1984.

The earliest Navajo rock art in Chaco, dating from about 1720 to 1750, is represented by a very few sites in the ceremonial Gobernador style. These sites feature pecked or painted mythical and religious subjects such as ye'i, or deities, the males dressed in kilts and the females in mantas. Other figures are incised but again include ceremonial images such as ye'i, shields (some of them horned and feathered), and masks. There is some suggestion, however, that these incised drawings are later in date than their pecked or painted counterparts. The incised ye'i are usually angular and elongated, resembling those found in modern sandpaintings. Representations of deer and bison, as well as hand and moccasin prints, also appear in this Navajo rock art.

The fifty-year interruption in Navajo occupation of Chaco Canyon probably marked the end of the representation of sacred subjects. Later rock art, including some from the twentieth century, often depicts human participants in ceremonies, but not the gods themselves. There are a few finely incised and painted groups of ye'i-bi-chai dancers, as well as several scenes of squaw dances and other social events, in which the women

Detail of an incised drawing of participants in a Navajo squaw dance, probably early twentieth century. The central woman wears a fringed shawl and carries a rattlestick wand; the men wear long robes and broad-brimmed hats. Photo by David Noble, 1984.

wear fringed blankets and long skirts, and the men, robes and broad-brimmed hats. The latter scenes also include hogans, wagons, and even trucks.

Following the Gobernador phase, horses became a major element in Navajo rock art. Stiffly modeled, elongated horses with pinnate tails, their manes indicated by rows of vertical lines, were incised into the cliffs and boulders of Chaco before 1800. Sometimes these animals are ridden by triangular- (later hourglass-) shaped men, who may carry lances, bows and arrows, and shields: Such scenes represent mythological, war, and hunting themes. Figures of horses became progressively more curvilinear as time went on, and as Navajo rock artists were influenced by Anglo standards through schooling and popular media, their work grew increasingly naturalistic. Eventually horses' manes and tails were shown as flowing, and horses were pictured in pastoral scenes integrated by ground lines.

The trend toward naturalism, and simultaneously toward the depiction of everyday events and objects, is noticeable in the treatment of other subjects as well. Trucks, cars, trains, and gable-roofed houses were all occasionally portrayed in rock art by later Navajos.

Testimony of the most recent phase of Chacoan history is provided by many incised and scratched inscriptions. These names, initials, brands, dates, and even unreadable groups of letters make up a large number of the canyon's historic "rock art" sites. Though some inscriptions may be the work of Navajos, most were made by nineteenth- and twentieth-century Anglo and Hispanic visitors. Some of the earliest Anglo inscriptions were carved by members of military expeditions in the mid-1800s, but

Late-eighteenth-or early-nineteenth-century incised Navajo horse. Photo by David Noble, 1984.

Inscriptions scratched on the cliff near a campsite on a late-nineteenth-century route through Chaco Canyon. Photo by David Noble, 1984.

most are somewhat later. Travelers passing through the canyon en route between Albuquerque and Farmington or Durango were responsible for many of them. The majority of the inscriptions, however, were the work of Hispanic sheepherders from the Chama Valley who brought their flocks into the region during the winter months from about 1900 to 1941. These herders frequently carved their names, the names of their towns and villages, and the date at sheep camps and herding stations.

The centuries-long graphic record at Chaco includes imagery reflecting myths, ideologies, and ceremonies of the Anasazis and Navajos, and perhaps even Anasazi calendrical practices. More recently, numerous graffiti speak for the varied groups who passed through the area. The canyon walls themselves are a vital document of Chaco's past.

Polly Schaafsma is a rock art specialist whose most recent book is *Indian Rock Art of the Southwest*. She is also an artist.

Archaeoastronomy at Chaco Canyon
The Historic-Prehistoric Connection

Michael Zeilik

HOW MUCH ASTRONOMY did prehistoric people know? Archaeoastronomy aims to answer this question. To do so properly, however, requires an investigation that unites astronomy, archaeology, and ethnography so that possible prehistoric astronomical sites are interpreted in the appropriate cultural context.

At Chaco, we hope to find out about the astronomy of prehistoric times. Archaeologists have worked extensively at this site and recently astronomers have also become involved. Their separate findings are now being synthesized to form a new view of Anasazi life.

If we can view them in the proper cultural context, the stone and adobe ruins of Chaco provide some insight into the life of the Anasazis. Key to this insight is the surviving astronomy of the historic pueblos. Their culture serves as a guide—and a caution—to interpreting possible Anasazi astronomical activities. While many pueblos disappeared beginning in 1540, those that survive are the direct cultural connection to the Anasazis.

Sunrise at Chaco Canyon. Horizon features can be used as solar calendrical markers. Photo by Michael Zeilik, 1983.

The Hopi pueblos in Arizona and Zuni in New Mexico provide the best clues to the past because these villages were touched only lightly by the Spaniards, in contrast to the submission demanded of those along the Rio Grande. The Hopi and Zuni pueblos preserve a remarkable continuity with the culture of prehistory.

The goal, then, is to "get into the skins" of the Anasazi Sun Priests by first studying their cultural heirs. Thus, we are forced partly out of necessity to argue by ethnographic analogy. This analogy provides some foundation for making connections with the past because we know that continuity rather than discontinuity appears to be central to the nature of Pueblo culture. Even when disruptions unhinge Pueblo societies, the force of tradition can preserve essential ideas. For example, even though the person who served as the Sun Priest at Zuni left the pueblo and died outside it in the 1950s, sun-watching activity is still carried out there. It is performed in the ways described at the beginning of this century, but by a new person in a different religious office. However, cultural changes do occur in the pueblos, especially in modern times, so analogy must be used with great caution.

SOLAR ASTRONOMY OF THE PUEBLOS

At Hopi and Zuni, astronomy plays a central role in agricultural and ceremonial life. The seasonal cycle of the sun sets the ritual calendar and determines the times of specific crop plantings. The dry southwestern climate demands observant farming, for raising crops is a risky and central activity—a matter of life or death until recent decades. So solar astronomy carries weight as both a practical and a religious function. Ritual and religion were probably born of the need for successful crops; sun watching was crucial to fulfilling that need.

Solar observation is invested in a religious officer, usually called the Sun Priest. He watches daily from a special spot within the pueblo or not far outside of it, carefully observing the position of sunrise or sunset relative to features on the horizon. He knows from experience which horizon points mark the summer and winter solstices and the times to plant crops. These he announces within the pueblo, usually ahead of time so that ritual and planting preparations can be carried out.

Along with horizon features, the Zunis and a few other Pueblos use windows and portholes in the pueblo that allow sunlight to hit special plates or markings on the walls at significant times of the year. Thus light and shadow, along with horizon features, constitute the basis of Pueblo solar astronomy. We expect that the same may have been true of Anasazi astronomy.

It is critical in Pueblo astronomy that the Sun Priest anticipate ceremonials. Pueblo culture requires preparation time before a ceremony so that the participants will be in the proper frame of mind to ensure the rite's effectiveness. For example, the Sun Priest at Hopi announces the winter solstice ceremony publicly on December 10 or 11; he starts the sun watching for this announcement on December 6. In the historic pueblos, the anticipatory observations start two to four weeks before the end of the solstitial ceremony. The winter solstice ceremony—called *Soyal* at Hopi and *Itiwanna* at Zuni—marks the heart of the ritual year.

The need for anticipation time relates to the astronomical problem of predicting solstices. Because at these times the sun does not move on the horizon, naked-eye observation cannot reveal which day is the solstice. The best way to determine the day astronomically is to observe the sun before the solstice, while it is still moving observable amounts along the horizon. I estimate that the minimum solar motion marking the sun's progress against horizon features that is detectable with just the eye occurs a week before the solstice. Observations made two weeks before or earlier will be even more reliable. The sun watcher can then do a day count, perhaps using knots on a rope to keep a tally, and predict the date on which the solstice will occur. Of course, a few years of sun watching are required to establish the anticipation times for various horizon markers, but once established, the horizon calendar remains fixed, and the knowledge can be passed on to others.

Because anticipatory observations play such a crucial part in the rituals at present-day pueblos, it may be deduced that a prehistoric site should work for both confirmatory and anticipatory observations if it is to be judged to have had an intentional observatory or calendrical function. If the site only confirms an astronomical event, the case for its intentional use is much weakened. The importance of anticipatory use of a site is illustrated by one practical example: low clouds might linger on the horizon in the winter and block out the sun's appearance, but it still would take only one anticipatory observation and a day count based on it for the Sun Priest to predict the solstice date within a day or two.

ANASAZI SUN WATCHING AT CHACO CANYON

A possible prehistoric sun site must be judged in terms of astronomy and ethnography, and also in archaeological terms. Archaeologists will ask crucial questions: Has the site been reconstructed? Is there a chance it has been disturbed? Do cultural artifacts in the vicinity give it a firm context? All these lines of evidence must point in favor of the astronomical intent of the builders.

Astronomical and ethnographic aspects of the study of Chaco sites are influenced by evidence that the Chacoans faced climatic conditions similar to those of today. Thus, we expect that their agricultural situation was much like that of the historic Pueblo

Corner windows like this one at Pueblo Bonito may have been used for anticipatory calendrical observations. Photo by Michael Zeilik, 1983.

In October, the sun begins to throw a narrow beam of light through a corner window onto the wall of this room at Pueblo Bonito. Photo by Michael Zeilik, 1983.

people and that they also had Sun Priests and seasonal solar calendars. However, horizon calendars based on natural features leave behind no artifacts. Further, the horizon from within and on top of the canyon presents a flat vista not useful for this type of calendar. Therefore, we expect that sites for light and shadow manipulation, especially within buildings, are the most likely sun-watching places to survive—and to be identifiable as such.

At Chaco, at least three places for sun watching using the light and shadow method may have existed: Pueblo Bonito, Casa Rinconada, and Fajada Butte. All contain some evidence in art or architecture that indicates possible sun-watching stations, although the data are more supportive for some sites than for others.

Pueblo Bonito has a number of corner doorways and windows, which are rather unusual in Anasazi architecture; in fact, it contains over half of the known examples of such openings. Archaeologist Jonathan Reyman noted that two of the windows in the southeastern part of the ruin offer a clear view of the winter solstice sunrise (provided that an outer wall did not obstruct the view). Both windows may also be used for anticipatory observations. They are fairly large, giving angular views of a few degrees to a person standing against the room's opposite wall. The viewer can move about two meters south and still see sky before the jambs block the view. At winter solstice, the sun rises in just about the middle of the opening. Approximately seven weeks before the winter solstice, the rising sun's light first enters one room through the jamb alignment and throws a narrow beam within. As the sun moves southward, the beam widens and moves northward over 1.5 meters. That gives an average motion

of about three centimeters per day, an easy amount to use in predicting the winter solstice.

The author has recently noticed that, when viewed from the east side of Pueblo Bonito, the horizon presents sufficient features to serve as a horizon calendar at sunrise. But these features flatten out to the southwest, and the horizon fails as a marker at the end of October, providing no clear indicator for the winter solstice. However, at just the time that the horizon calendar fails, sunlight first appears in one corner window opening. It may be surmised that the failure of the horizon calendar to predict and confirm the winter solstice might have led the Chacoans to incorporate the special openings in Pueblo Bonito.

Casa Rinconada lies directly across the canyon from Pueblo Bonito. Archaeologists believe it was a great kiva used for community ceremonies or activities. It is almost thirty meters in diameter, one of the largest kivas known. A person standing in its center can see a window in the northeast corner. On the morning of the summer solstice, about a half-hour after sunrise, a beam of sunlight will pass through the window and strike one of six niches that are spaced irregularly around the inside wall of the kiva. As the sun climbs the sky, the ray moves downward until it hits the floor. The beam strikes the niche for about a week at the time of the summer solstice.

Although this effect is visually dramatic, the author has doubts as to whether it was intended by the Anasazis. First, the kiva has been reconstructed, and neither the exact location of the original opening nor its overall size is known. (It is, however, clear from photos taken before the reconstruction that an opening did exist in the northeast side.) Second, a wall or room outside the

As the winter solstice nears, the same beam of light widens and moves northward along the wall. Tracking this ray, an observer could anticipate the solstice and plan ceremonies in advance. Photo by Michael Zeilik, 1983.

On the winter solstice, a beam of light strikes a niche in the wall of Casa Rinconada. Photo by Michael Zeilik, 1981.

window may have blocked out the sunlight. Third, kivas have roofs, and in Casa Rinconada stone circles mark the positions of the four massive posts needed to support the heavy roof. The one in the northwest corner seems to just block the sunlight from hitting the niche on the summer solstice. Fourth, in the historic pueblos, kivas are not used for sun watching, although the stars are observed from them. Overall, the author judges that evidence for the use of the site as an astronomical observatory by the Anasazis is shaky at best.

Fajada Butte thrusts upward at the eastern end of the canyon—the lone dramatic break in the landscape. Atop the butte is a sun marker that tracks the seasons. Within ten meters of the summit, three rock slabs lie against the butte's southeast face. The slabs are a few meters long, with gaps of about ten centimeters between them. They shield the rock face on which they rest from the sun except at times before local solar noon. Then the edges of the slabs allow sunlight to strike the rock face, on which are carved two spirals: a large one, almost one-half meter wide, right behind the slabs, and a smaller one below and to the left of the first.

The spirals mark the sun's yearly cycle by light patterns visible late in the morning. On the summer solstice, a shaft of light materializes above the large spiral at about 11:00 A.M. In approximately twenty minutes, it descends and slices through the heart of the spiral design. (At the summer solstice, this beam of light suggests the "dagger" often mentioned in reference to the site; however, at other times of the year its appearance is simply that of a shaft of light.) On the winter solstice, a shaft of light appears on each side of the large spiral and passes through its outer edges at about 10:00 A.M. At both equinoxes, two shafts appear, one shorter than and to the left of the other. The little shaft cuts through the center of the small spiral, while the big one drops through one side of the large spiral.

Is this a formation that the Anasazis intended for calendrical solar observations? The slabs are the result of a natural rockfall; they were not moved to their present location. People of the historic pueblos tend to use natural features, with little modification, for sun watching. The spirals may have been placed behind the slabs after the natural play of light was noted for a year. The fact that the shafts appear in the late morning, not a particularly significant time of day, reinforces the view that the rocks were in a natural formation. The site certainly does confirm the solstices and equinoxes in a visually stunning way.

However, there are problems with this as a calendrical site; these relate to the cultural context. First, almost all sun-watching stations of historic pueblos are within or close to the pueblo. Fajada Butte is more than a kilometer distant from the nearest Chacoan greathouse and is hard to climb. Pueblos on or around the butte either postdate Chaco's abandonment or are small villages of five to fifteen rooms. The Fajada Butte petroglyph spirals would have been a rather impractical station for daily sun watching, especially in winter, when snow and ice can coat the sheer chimney that is the only access to the top. Second, spirals are not yet known to be sun symbols in historic Pueblo culture; they are most commonly interpreted as water signs or migration symbols. Why are they used here? Were spirals connected to the sun in prehistoric times? Finally, the site does not work

On the summer solstice, a shaft of light splits the large petroglyph spiral on Fajada Butte. Photo by Karl Kernberger, 1978.

The three rock slabs of the Fajada Butte sun marker. The hat at lower right indicates scale. Photo by Michael Zeilik, 1983.

for "precise" anticipatory observations—that is, it is not accurate within a day. During the month before the summer solstice, the main shaft of sunlight moves horizontally on the average only a millimeter per day, a motion too small to detect by eye and much smaller than the width of the shaft and the pecking of the spirals. This site fails the anticipatory test; it is the only one of the three discussed here that does so. Although the hypothesis is tempting, the Fajada Butte site is not yet well proven as an intentional construct of the Anasazis for calendrical sun-watching purposes. The author is more inclined to view it as a possible sun shrine, to which the Sun Priest traveled on an occasional basis to pray and deposit offerings. It has many of the same attributes as historic sun shrines, especially those investigated by J. W. Fewkes at Hopi at the end of the last century: it is formed of a pile of rocks, is marked by petroglyphs, and is located on the top of a mesa some distance from the nearest pueblo.

It is hoped that this excursion through some of the archaeo-astronomical sites at Chaco gives the reader a flavor of Anasazi astronomy—a taste that can also be sampled at the historic pueblos. Perhaps it has conveyed as well a sense of the uncertainty under which archaeoastronomy operates. We can never really know whether our ideas are correct; but we can, if we are careful, develop at least a broad template to aid in our understanding of cultures so far from us in time. To do so, we must heed the cultural guide from the historic pueblos. To be of any use to archaeology and anthropology in the Southwest in general and at Chaco in particular, archaeoastronomy must progress from simply finding alignments to discovering the uses of these sites in the proper cultural context.

Michael Zeilik is associate professor of astronomy at the University of New Mexico and has written *Astronomy: The Evolving Universe* and *Astronomy: The Cosmic Perspective*. He has conducted extensive archaeo-astronomical research at Anasazi and Pueblo sites in the Southwest.

The Chaco Navajos

David M. Brugge

Navajos from the Chaco area enjoy a meal at the Hyde Expedition's kitchen behind Pueblo Bonito, 1896. Courtesy American Museum of Natural History.

ALL ROADS led to the Chaco Canyon villages. There was frequent travel over these roads, on which sandal prints left indications of journeys in both directions until the winds obscured them or new ones were imprinted on the old. In time, more tracks led out of the canyon than inward. Soon few tracks were left on the roads, and the winds that periodically swept the sands clean erased little more than signs of passage by wild animals. At long intervals, perhaps, the impressions of one or a few pairs of sandals would appear, but vegetation had begun to invade the old roadways.

How long this desolate condition lasted we do not know. The grasses grew thicker along the former routes, and game increased. Herds of antelope roamed the plains, and in the higher, wooded, and rougher country, deer became more common. When the tracks of human beings once again appeared, they looked different, and they did not follow the old roads so faithfully. These new prints, left by moccasins, tended to favor the narrow game trails. And when the winter snows lay deep, snowshoe tracks could be found.

The new people were probably few and highly mobile. They were hunters of game and gatherers of wild crops: grass seeds, berries, nuts, and fruits. Whatever the land produced, they harvested, traveling great distances from one ripening to another. The women or the people's dogs carried the few goods that they possessed, while the men walked armed with strong bows, ready to repel attack or bag any game so unwary as to be seen. Where the sandal-wearers had built pueblos, cleared fields, and laid out roads, the moccasin-wearers trod lightly, leaving little to mark their brief campsites.

This is about as much as we can safely say regarding the arrival of the Apacheans in the San Juan Basin. There is little evidence to suggest that they helped drive out the Anasazis, but it seems logical to assume that the Apacheans did not delay too long in moving into the abandoned regions, for other peoples would have preempted the land had they not arrived first.

Spreading southward and westward from the headwaters of

Navajos making mats from corn husks. The Navajos adopted maize agriculture from their Pueblo neighbors soon after entering the Southwest. Courtesy Museum of New Mexico (neg. 11988).

the Rio Grande and the San Juan River, Apacheans soon filled much or all of the country abandoned by the ancient agriculturists. One group, known as the *Apaches de Nabajo,* learned something about farming. With a more secure economic base, these people were able to increase in numbers more rapidly than the others.

In the 1500s, other peoples arrived from the opposite direction. This new migration was led by Spaniards, but some people of Indian descent were also among them. A few demonstrations of Spanish military might were sufficient to convince the pueblo dwellers that they should submit to foreign rule. While the neighboring Apacheans coveted the obvious wealth of the Hispanic intruders and hoped to learn how to gain the blessings of the Christian supernaturals, they were unwilling to surrender their freedom for such unproven advantages. The Spaniards had metal tools and weapons, gunpowder, and the magical power of writing, but the Apacheans could easily observe that with these boons also came new diseases, which struck with greater mortality in the towns than among their own scattered bands. Certain other innovations were denied Indians living under Spanish rule but were soon available to the free tribes. The most significant of these was the horse, which adapted so well to its new environment that tribal peoples who had relatively little experience with this animal could succeed in raising herds of their own.

ASSIMILATION OF REFUGEES

The free tribes did not escape the ravages of Old World epidemic diseases, of course, and the Apachean population declined almost as rapidly as did the Puebloans. Their dispersed, small settlements and practice of avoiding the dead gave only limited protection. The real key to tribal survival was probably the influx of refugees, who included both remnants of decimated bands and lone fugitives from Spanish rule.

Individuals or small groups might desert to join the free tribes with little notice. On occasion, large groups might flee, although these were pursued by armed men. Plots to drive out the intruders soon developed, usually in concert with the Apaches, who would time their raids to coincide with Puebloan resistance. Such attempts were generally futile. However, in 1680, after more than eight decades of restless submission, sufficient unity had developed among the diverse Pueblos and their Apachean allies to enable the Indians to drive out the whites. The victory was not to be permanent, however. When a forceful governor, Don Diego de Vargas, led Hispanic forces northward twelve years later, the reconquest grew on the crumbling ruins of a transitory unity.

As capitulation and disaster spread, the earlier strategy of flight to join the free tribes became the only solution for those most devoted to the cause of the revolt. By traversing the eastern mountains to reach the Plains Apaches or by crossing the Conti-

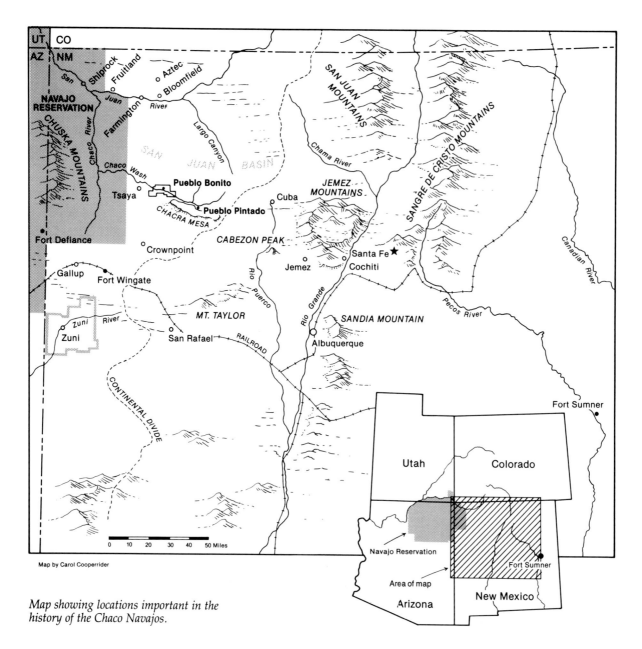

Map showing locations important in the history of the Chaco Navajos.

nental Divide to the west to live among the Navajos and Hopis, many were able to escape Spanish vengeance, at least temporarily. Enough stayed permanently among the Navajos and Hopis to change the course of events in the West dramatically.

The first Pueblos to join the Navajos were probably Tewa or Keres people who settled along the San Juan River and up Largo Canyon, east of present-day Farmington. They had been driven from their homes by de Vargas's victories at the mesa of Cochiti and at Black Mesa in the summer of 1694. By 1696, the crushing of a second revolt resulted in the arrival of Jemez refugees.

The Chaco country did not attract Puebloan refugees, but a few scattered Navajo families may still have been wandering in the area. Once they had established themselves in the northeastern part of the Apacheans' country, however, the Pueblos raised corn in such abundance and sponsored ceremonies of such power that the dispersed Navajos were attracted in large numbers to the vicinity. The refugees probably hoped to draw together so many people that they could return to central New Mexico as liberators, but that was not to be. Warfare endured for some two decades with neither side gaining any decisive advantage. Then a new enemy became a threat both to the Spaniards and their subjects and to the Navajos.

The Utes, often accompanied by their allies and linguistic cousins, the Comanches, had long been occasional adversaries of the Navajos and some of the Pueblos. They had found the Spaniards willing allies and customers for their trade in loot and captives. Perhaps it was their Comanche relatives who upset this arrangement. In any case, growing Ute hostility and aggressiveness gave the Navajos and Spaniards a common enemy.

By this time, the original refugees were growing old, their children were marrying Navajo spouses, and the lingua franca of all had become Navajo. The Pueblos' linguistic and political identity had been lost, but the assimilation of their way of life was bringing about a cultural florescence in the country along the upper San Juan. This development would remake the Navajo Tribe into something never before seen—an Indian group prospering as a result of a pastoral economy.

DINETAH AND CHACRA MESA

As the population grew in this region, which acquired the name *Dinetah* ("among the Navajos"), a few of the people moved southward, perhaps to find better fields and pastures, perhaps to escape the raids of Utes and Comanches. The earliest sites of this Navajo complex to appear outside of the Dinetah are found along the northeastern flank of Chacra Mesa, a formation extending southeast from Chaco Canyon. Some of these may date as early as the 1720s. Pueblitos (small pueblos), an architectural concept introduced by the refugees, were built in defensive locations, while hogans, the indigenous Navajo dwellings, appeared both near the pueblitos and in less defensive, but well hidden, places at higher elevations. By the 1740s, there were several such settlements on Chacra Mesa. At about this time, Spanish settlers were also expanding out of the Rio Grande Valley, and by the 1740s were intruding into the eastern part of Navajo country, gaining a welcome by promising to help drive off Ute raiders.

In the early 1750s, the Ute-Comanche pressure combined with drought and growing internal discord to force a near abandonment of the Dinetah. Even this situation did not lead immediately to a rupture in the long peace between the Navajos and Spaniards, but it did place strains on the relationship as the desperate Navajos helped swell the burgeoning population to the south. Navajo herds were also growing—a necessary adaptation when drought and warfare made farming a less secure means of feeding a family. Competition for land between Indians and

A Navajo woman at the doorway of her hogan. Photo by Gustaf Nordenskiold, 1891, courtesy New Mexico State Records Center and Archives, Wagner Collection.

whites grew slowly but steadily. The break came in 1773, when the Spanish governor in Santa Fe formed an alliance with the Utes. In the next year, the Navajos drove the white colonists out of their settlements all along the Rio Puerco of the East and around Mount Taylor. Details of the war are not known, but it is probable that Spanish troops campaigned in the Chacra country. Following the war, there was continued Navajo occupation of the Chaco region.

The emigrants from the Dinetah in the 1750s appear to have been influenced by religious values that were part of a revitalization movement. Probably the theology of the Pueblo Revolt still exerted sufficient influence to partially support this religious movement, and a reassertion of old Apachean values is also apparent in the lifeways of the people at this time. Blessingway became the dominant ceremony; it propounded a return to a simple way of life. The Anasazis had built pueblos and made elaborately decorated pottery—and they were now gone. It seemed wise, then, that the Navajos, facing a threat to their own existence, give up Pueblo-style architecture and painted pottery. The people must be willing to move whenever drought, enemies, or ill fortune struck. Such was the gods' apparent decree, and many accepted the teachings of the singers of Blessingway, although some still clung to the old ways. Many of the late-eighteenth-century Navajo homesites on Chacra Mesa indicate a reluctance to make great changes. The Ute raids were probably less severe for them, and the need to alter their ways perhaps not as strongly felt.

The successes of the war of 1774–75 may have reinforced the Navajos' faith in the old customs. Then in 1781 came an event that some of them may well have regarded as Spanish vengeance: one of the worst smallpox epidemics on record swept through New Mexico, causing many deaths among the Pueblos. At least one Navajo was baptized by a Spanish missionary as a result of this pestilence, but we have no documentation of its spread into Navajo country. However, a sudden decrease in hogan construction on Chacra Mesa strongly suggests that the devastation did spread well beyond the boundaries of the Spanish colony.

INCURSIONS INTO THE CHACO COUNTRY

Occupation of the Chaco country in the late 1700s was sparse. The area had become a buffer zone between more densely occupied country to the south and west and the homes of old enemies, such as the Utes and Comanches and the newly hostile Hispanics.

Into the 1800s, warfare between the Navajos and the New Mexicans escalated steadily. Chacra Mesa appears to have become an outpost, a staging area for raids and peace missions into the colony on the east, and a base camp for hunting parties. It seems probable that lookouts were posted there at dangerous times so that herds could be moved to safety well before the arrival of enemy troops. A few families living at strategic locations made it possible for the tribe to maintain an early warning system, even during less precarious periods.

By the end of Spanish rule in Mexico in 1821, if not earlier, it is probable that Chaco Canyon was a major military campaign route into Navajo country. Facundo Melgares, governor of New Mexico under both the Spanish and Mexican flags, led expeditions against the Navajos in 1818 and 1819. In 1821 and again in 1822, he sent other colonists against the Navajos. That some of these followed the Chaco River seems almost certain.

In 1823, when José Antonio Vizcarra led the first well-documented expedition down the canyon, he recorded a full set of Spanish place names with no suggestion that he was applying them for the first time. It is unlikely that his failure to claim credit for naming the landmarks along his route was the result of modesty. The available evidence suggests that Blas de Hinojos's disastrous campaign of 1835 also marched down the Chaco.

By 1849, Colonel John Macrae Washington's march, so ably recorded by Lieutenant James H. Simpson and illustrated by the Kern brothers, benefited from the knowledge of guides. The Navajos who dealt with the expedition were experienced in watching troops follow west a route long used by invaders of their territory.

The initial efforts of U.S. officials in dealing with the Navajos were not much more effective than those of their Spanish and Mexican predecessors. The whites might have continued the same indecisive alternation between war and peace for decades had not the Civil War, which began fifteen years after the U.S. occupation of New Mexico, occasioned a build-up of troops. A Confederate invasion of the Territory was so decisively defeated by Union forces in 1862 that no second attempt was made by the South. Because New Mexico's location was the key to the gold deposits in California and Colorado, a substantial garrison was maintained there throughout the rest of the war. The presence of a large number of troops made campaigns against the neighboring tribes more feasible than at any earlier time. The Navajos, one of the largest free tribes in the West, became an early target.

In 1863, General James Carleton sent the Navajos an ultimatum, requiring in effect that they surrender and submit to removal from their country or face war. When no Navajos appeared, Kit Carson was sent out. He had less than a thousand men under his command, but he had two permanent posts, old Fort Wingate near present-day San Rafael and Fort Canby, the modern Fort Defiance. In addition, all other tribes that could be persuaded to fight against the Navajos soon had warriors in the field. Hispanic raiders followed not far behind. In the 1860s, more captive Navajo women and children were baptized in the village churches of New Mexico than ever before. In the winter of 1863–64, Navajos surrendered in large numbers and were sent to Fort Sumner on the Pecos River.

Navajos under military guard at Fort Sumner. Courtesy U.S. Army Signal Corps collections in the Museum of New Mexico (neg. 28534).

There is a tradition in the Chaco country that army wagons came to Pueblo Pintado to help transport people into exile, although the date and commander of such an expedition are unknown. The families living in the Chaco area prior to their exile had been poor and possessed little livestock. As a consequence, the native vegetation was not much disturbed by grazing, and game was relatively plentiful. The land appears to have remained entirely uninhabited during the absence of the Navajos. Although the Chaco region was left outside of the reservation created by treaty in 1868, the year the Navajos were allowed to return to their homeland, families soon moved back to their original ranges.

SETTLERS, TRADERS, AND ARCHAEOLOGISTS

Settlers did not move into eastern Navajo country until the following decade. After an absence of almost a century, Hispanics returned to Cabezon in 1870 and to San Luis, La Ventana, and Cuba in 1872. Farther north, Anglo homesteaders founded Farmington in 1876, Fruitland in 1878, and Aztec in 1880, not long after the arrival of Hispanic settlers at Bloomfield in 1872. Rosa was first settled in 1878.

This influx was around the periphery of the Chaco country, but the stockmen of the new communities soon began to penetrate the hinterland. Unsubstantiated reports place the LC and Carlisle cattle companies in the Chaco area by 1878 or 1879. Sheepmen were nearby in 1882, and by 1884, sheep ranching by the Miera brothers of Cuba had been extended to the vicinity of Chaco Canyon and complaints from Navajos and whites over rights to rangeland were beginning.

Also in the 1880s, traders were moving beyond the rivers and the already settled country to do business with the Navajos. In 1885, a Mr. Haynes established the post of Tiz-na-zin ten miles west of Pueblo Bonito, and by 1889, one Thomas Hye was trading at Pueblo Pintado. Both traders in the countryside and some of those in the settlements gave moral support to Navajo resistance to the whites who were occupying their lands—and sometimes the support was more than moral. By 1883, the Navajos were reported to be well supplied with firearms, including up-to-date Winchesters and plenty of ammunition. In addition, some had learned directly from professional soldiers how to use the new weapons. And service as army scouts in the Apache campaigns had brought them valuable contacts with government representatives, who would not oppose their right to graze their herds on land in the public domain and would often give them additional backing.

Most important, however, even the federal government in Washington, D.C., recognized Indian rights to the peaceful use of public lands. Indian agents were charged with enforcing this right but lacked the resources to do so and were sometimes faced with conflicting requirements that undermined their efforts. The Navajos seldom tried to challenge whites directly on this issue, because they recognized the necessity of avoiding another war such as the one that had resulted in their exile.

When thirty armed whites came to drive them from the Chaco area in 1890, they left without resistance. The exact location of this incident, the number of Navajos dispossessed, and the identity of their assailants remain unknown, but it seems unlikely that the Indians permanently relocated. Despite occasional attempts by government agents to require Navajos to live on the reservation, the agents' tendency was to ignore what they could not control. Government officials increasingly supported the Navajos' rights outside the reservation. In 1893, agent E. H. Plummer issued several permits, some to Chaco people, to leave the reservation to gather salt, hunt, and engage in wage work. In the following year, he began to write permits for Navajos who claimed land, including two prominent men from Chaco, Welo and Navajo George. (Plummer's spelling of the Navajos' Spanish and English names was hindered by their Navajo accents, but even as *Way-low* and *Choge* they are recognizable.)

In 1895, the canyon was visited by Richard Wetherill, who was acting as guide for the Palmer family. A daughter of the family, Marietta, who later married Wetherill, has provided most of the information we have on this visit. At the time, Navajos lived all around the canyon and herded their sheep into it. Hispanic herders were also present, camping at the ruins and bedding their sheep in the shelter of the old walls.

Wetherill returned in 1896 with George H. Pepper to commence archaeological excavations financed by the wealthy Hyde brothers of New York. The project, which was called the Hyde Exploring Expedition, gave the local Navajo men what was prob-

The interior of a typical trading post on the Navajo reservation in 1949. Photo by Milton Snow, courtesy Museum of New Mexico (neg. 46809).

ably their first experience with wage work. In addition, their wives found Pepper an eager purchaser of their woven blankets. He soon had them producing runners, pillow tops, and even the first sandpainting tapestry. The visitors also rented a stove from Welo.

Because Navajo workers encountered difficulties in cashing their paychecks at nearby trading posts, the expedition began to pay the workmen in groceries during the second season of work in 1897. This development led to the opening of a small trading post that fall by the Wetherills, and the enterprise was enlarged the following summer as a joint venture by Richard Wetherill and the Hyde brothers. There is a suggestion that the enterprising newcomers also began to raise sheep about this time, an endeavor that would have placed them in direct competition with their Navajo customers for grazing rights.

Pressure from whites increased during this period, and accusations of theft and trespass were made by both sides. Anglos were gaining control of the sheep business. Two of them, T. D. Burns and his nephew Edward Sargent of the Chama region, were also major political powers in New Mexico. Their herders were still Hispanic, and the old pattern of bringing sheep from the Chama Valley to the Chaco country for the winter continued.

About the turn of the century, the Hydes and Richard Wetherill began to expand their trading business rapidly. In February 1900, they were reported to own eight trading posts. By April they had thirteen, and an additional four stores were probably acquired during that same year.

Opposition to the expedition's operations grew. Professor Edgar L. Hewett protested that the archaeological work done in 1900 was mere vandalism. This objection was prompted in part, perhaps, by the fact that no professional archaeologist had been hired to replace Pepper, who did not return after 1899. The Wetherills continued archaeological explorations on their own. Catholic priests at Saint Michael's Mission made complaint of Wetherill's dealings with the Navajos, and from some unknown source there was even an accusation that he was drilling oil wells.

While some of the charges appear to be exaggerated, there is clear evidence that Wetherill was quite arbitrary in his methods of debt collection and was alienating Navajo sympathies in this regard at least. His livestock holdings also appear to have been large enough to create growing conflict over range rights with both local Navajos and Hispanic herders from the Chama region.

LAND STATUS

Land status in the Chaco country was ill defined. The federal government had given sections for fifty miles from the railroad right-of-way to the south as a railway grant to help stimulate the development of a transcontinental rail system. This fifty-mile zone extended to Chaco Canyon. The even-numbered sections and the lands beyond to the north were in the public domain.

The potential for conflict in this situation is readily apparent. Both Anglos and Hispanics felt that they had rights to preempt any seemingly unoccupied lands, while Indians believed that their long if sporadic use of the land was sanctioned by their gods. In order to avoid war, methods of establishing legal rights to the land had to be applied.

Although the railroad lands had a legal status, most were used as freely as the public domain, even at the beginning of the twentieth century. It is uncertain just when stockmen began to lease or buy land from the railroad to improve their claims to range, for the railroad was no more able than the federal government to control the use of its more remote lands during these early years.

The first record of such efforts appears in 1901. Richard Wetherill and Frederick Hyde both claimed homestead tracts in Chaco Canyon at that time, and Marietta Wetherill reportedly purchased three sections of railroad land. It appears that the Wetherills and Hyde took these actions on their own initiative.

The earliest documented government action relating to land in the Chaco region was a temporary withdrawal in 1905 of two townships plus two additional sections in order to protect some of the ruins. In the following year, an allotting agent was assigned

Navajos congregate at the Wetherill trading post at Pueblo Bonito for a celebration, September 1899. Photo by George Pepper, courtesy New Mexico State Records Center and Archives, McNitt Collection.

the duty of surveying 160-acre allotments for individual Navajos living east of the reservation. It was not until 1907 that a national monument was formally created to preserve the ruins. Toward the end of that same year, a temporary extension of the reservation was made. Agent William H. Harrison at Fort Defiance recommended that the federal government try to restrain the railroad's leasing and selling of land to white ranchers because many Indians had unknowingly built their homes on railroad sections.

Bureau of Indian Affairs (BIA) officials realized that the reservation extension would be short lived. The allotting program was pushed as rapidly as resources permitted with the aim of placing most water sources in the eastern area in Navajo ownership, thereby giving the Indians control of most of the grazing land as well, a strategy that white ranchers had long used elsewhere to control rangelands.

In addition, a new superintendency was created. It took several months to fill the new position, but by April 12, 1909, Samuel F. Stacher had assumed his duties as superintendent at Pueblo Bonito, where he intended to build a new school, oversee the well-being of most of the eastern Navajos, and defend their rights to land. He initially rented office space and quarters from Richard Wetherill.

It did not take long for Stacher to realize that Wetherill's interests conflicted with those of the people under his charge. He found himself in an increasingly serious controversy with Wetherill and his employees. Besides Wetherill's arbitrary methods of debt collection and competition with the Navajos for range,

The herding of sheep and goats was a vital part of traditional Navajo economy. Photo by T. Harmon Parkhurst, about 1935, courtesy Museum of New Mexico (neg. 88867).

Stacher learned, his employees were involved in selling them liquor. While it appears that the Wetherills were not personally involved in this last activity, it obviously did not help smooth relations. Whether the subsequent removal of the superintendency from Chaco Canyon to Crownpoint was a direct result of these problems is not entirely clear.

THE KILLING OF RICHARD WETHERILL

Most Chaco Navajos had been involved in disputes of one sort or another with Wetherill. As early as Wetherill's second season of work in the canyon, old Welo found him ready to draw a gun merely to retain use of his rented stove—even though Welo had wished only to retrieve it temporarily for use during a ceremony. Navajo George, one of the oldest and wealthiest stockmen in the area, had a long-standing dispute with Wetherill over a debt allegedly incurred by George's late wife.

The year 1910 was marked by drastic events. In February or March, Wetherill sold his trading post, apparently to one of the Miera brothers of Cuba. In time, he leased his grazing land to Tom Talle, a rancher from Gallup. While Richard Wetherill was helping Talle drive his cattle to Chaco Canyon, a Wetherill employee, Will Finn, rode west to take possession of a horse at Antonio Padilla's hogan. There are widely varying stories today as to who owned the horse, why Padilla had it, and why Finn went to get it. In any case, the disagreement that arose over the ownership of the horse led to much more dramatic events.

Finn pistol-whipped Padilla and left him bleeding in front of his hogan. Padilla's wife sought the aid of her brother, Chiishch'ilin Biye', who helped move his brother-in-law into the shade of a nearby tree. Padilla appeared dead, although he was later revived. Chiishch'ilin Biye' then set out to avenge his brother-in-law's presumed death, stopping first at the trading post at Tsaya to buy ammunition for his rifle. He then rode to Pueblo Bonito, where he joined other Navajos in a gambling game. He might well have abandoned his mission at this point had not Wetherill and Finn stopped at the place where the Navajos were gambling. Wetherill engaged in an argument with Welo and Chiishch'ilin Biye', which the latter apparently interpreted as a threat on his life. Wetherill and Finn then rode west, behind the Talle herd. Chiishch'ilin Biye' also circled back to the west to retrieve his rifle, which he had cached at some distance from the game, and rode forth to accept the challenge. The Navajo urged his horse east this time, along the same road taken by the two whites. His only advantage in this encounter of two against one was the setting sun at his back.

The opponents saw each other at a distance of about 150 yards. The trader and his helper spurred their horses to a lope, and with curses and drawn guns charged the Navajo. Chiishch'ilin Biye' dismounted when the white men were within about 25

Wetherill's grave at Pueblo Bonito. Photo by David Noble, 1984.

yards. They exchanged several shots, and Wetherill fell from his horse. Chiishch'ilin Biye' then shot twice at Finn, who turned his horse and fled toward the Wetherill ranch house. After shooting Wetherill once more, Chiishch'ilin Biye' rode off to surrender to the superintendent at Shiprock, William T. Shelton. Behind him a group of frightened whites barricaded themselves in the ranch house, while their equally frightened Navajo neighbors sought safety on the mesa rims in camps that they had used in the days before Kit Carson.

INTO THE MODERN ERA

Wetherill's death did not greatly affect the course of events in the Chaco country. Other whites acquired his interests, and new homesteaders arrived with hopes of building up larger holdings. In 1911, the last portion of the eastern extension of the reservation was cancelled and the process of allotting land to the Navajos ceased not long after. Stacher's efforts on the Navajos' behalf amounted to holding actions. He relied on allotments, compromises with those ranchers most likely to respect Navajo rights, and leasing of railroad lands. His agreements with the white ranchers helped some of the Navajos, but they aroused opposition from those who had to sacrifice ancestral lands in order to make possible any continuing Navajo presence in the east. The political pressures from the white ranchers were so great that he had no alternative, however. One of these white ranchers, Edward Sargent, who was especially influential politically, was establishing his ranch immediately east of Chaco Canyon.

A shrinking land base and a growing population placed great strains on the eastern Navajo economy. At Chaco Canyon, the ruins of the Anasazi culture became one source of economic relief in 1921, when archaeological investigations were resumed. Edgar L. Hewett, who had played a prominent role in establishing the national monument and in opposing the work of the Hydes and of Wetherill, was in charge of one effort. In the same year, Neil Judd also began excavations under the auspices of the National Geographic Society. The jobs available at the excavations were very much needed by the Navajos.

Judd's fieldwork continued through 1927. Hewett, who had not excavated after 1921, returned in 1929 and developed a program involving the School of American Research, the Museum of New Mexico, and the University of New Mexico. This work continued for many years. In 1928, the National Park Service also began initial stabilization work at the ruins, employing mostly Navajos on the work crews. Then, in 1929, the first full-time custodian, Hilding F. Palmer, arrived, and park projects became more frequent providers of employment.

The Great Depression led to an increase in government programs of all kinds. In 1929, a new allotting agent was sent to the region. He was able to average about one hundred allotments per month for a little more than a year before the political pressures of white ranchers forced the suspension of his work.

Meanwhile, Stacher was actively promoting political organization of the Navajos in his jurisdiction through the establishment of chapters, a form of public meeting that the Bureau of Indian Affairs hoped would promote cultural change. A program to consolidate Navajo and white areas east of the reservation was begun in 1931, but white opposition doomed it to failure. At the same time, many young whites, unable to obtain employment, were moving into the region to homestead, hoping that dry-farming would prove a viable alternative. Neither the Navajos nor the white ranchers were happy to see them, but since most were veterans of World War I, overt resistance to this development would not have been politically expedient.

The deepening of the Depression brought a change in the federal administration in 1932. As soon as he became president, Franklin D. Roosevelt instituted many large-scale government programs to provide employment, with National Park Sevice projects receiving high priority. Many of the early projects at Chaco Canyon employed workers from distant places, including young non-Indians from Pennsylvania and Sioux from the Dakotas. However, the Bureau of Indian Affairs received separate funding for projects that hired local Navajos. In time, a special ruins stabilization unit was organized at the canyon under the direction of Gordon Vivian. The unit employed Navajos who had

The School of American Research, like other institutions working in Chaco Canyon, employed many Navajos as excavators. This crew is digging at Chetro Ketl. Courtesy Museum of New Mexico (neg. 66975).

The ruins stabilization unit, trained by Gordon Vivian, repairs the tower kiva at Kin Ya'a in about 1955. Courtesy National Park Service.

developed unusual skill at reproducing the prehistoric masonry styles in their repairs of crumbling walls. This crew worked not only on the canyon sites but increasingly on ruins throughout New Mexico and Arizona.

In spite of these economically beneficial projects, a different government undertaking created greater Navajo-white animosity than had any event since the Fort Sumner exile. Overgrazing had long been recognized by conservationists as harmful to western ranges, and conservation was a prominent theme in many of the projects established to stimulate the economy. Therefore, government-funded stock reduction programs were undertaken among the Navajo herds. These efforts were based on a practical knowledge of range management but revealed abysmal ignorance of the role livestock played in Navajo culture. The program's effects on Navajo attitudes toward whites were severe throughout Navajo country, and for the off-reservation Navajos a genuinely disastrous situation was created. As Navajo stock were removed by the government, white ranchers who were not subject to the same regulations brought in new animals to graze the range that the Navajos could no longer utilize fully.

Other measures to consolidate land in order to create separate Navajo and white areas had been only marginally successful, despite Stacher's most strenuous efforts. The new administration proposed a boundary bill to settle the matter by establishing an eastern extension of the reservation and leaving the rest of the country to white ranchers. BIA officials even promised the Navajos reservation status in exchange for voluntary stock reduction. When repeated efforts to get the bill through Congress failed, the eastern Navajos became the strongest opponents of government proposals within the tribe, defeating a planned reorganization of the tribal government in a hard-fought election and then helping elect as tribal chairman Jacob C. Morgan, the staunchest foe of federal programs among Navajo leaders of the period.

The Indian population was already under severe economic stress as a result of restricted access to grazing lands. The effects of stock reduction and consequent loss of additional land brought poverty of a sort that few Navajos had experienced for many years. Among the park projects was a fence for the boundary of the national monument. Once it was completed, the Navajos within the monument were required to move. The loss of range was keenly felt, and had the park not been a source of jobs, the results would probably have been catastrophic.

As had been true almost two centuries earlier, one source of hope came in the form of religious revelation. At least two women among the eastern Navajos had visions in which native supernaturals prescribed Blessingway ceremonies.

The difficult years did not end with the beginning of a new decade. Yet the fall of Threatening Rock onto Pueblo Bonito in January 1941 may be seen with hindsight as a positive omen.

After the Japanese attack on Pearl Harbor brought the United States into World War II, Navajo attitudes about the war varied to both extremes. One woman reported a vision that revealed that the Japanese were the sons of the Navajo gods and had come to kill the whites. On the other hand, many from the Ruins Stabilization Unit were ready to raid an oriental restaurant in Farmington until assured that the owners were not Japanese but Chinese. In time, the number of Navajos who served in the armed forces or worked in defense industries became so great that the tribe enjoyed renewed prosperity. Because of the demands for manpower, no custodian remained at the monument, and some of the Navajos evicted earlier moved back temporarily to their old homes. Again Blessingway ceremonies were held, this time to pray for the safety of young Navajos overseas.

The effects of World War II on the Navajos were longer lasting than simple wartime prosperity. Returning servicemen and war workers placed a sudden burden on the resources of the land, and the veterans were made dramatically aware of the production limits of their homeland. They also felt sharply the poor preparation they had received in school to compete for jobs. The crisis that followed the war was as serious for the Navajos as the effects of the Depression had been. A new understanding of the world beyond the tribe's four sacred mountains led to a readier acceptance of the importance of education and, within a few years, to a remarkable growth in schools and school attendance.

A present-day Navajo farmstead near Chaco Canyon. Photo by Paul Logsdon, 1982.

Oil discoveries, uranium mining, and the exploitation of other minerals brought a sudden increase in tribal wealth. A significant proportion of this money was used for scholarships. For the eastern Navajos, there was another gain. As the white ranchers aged, they sought to retire by selling the ranches that their children did not want. Perhaps the most important acquisition for the Chaco people was the 1958 purchase of the Sargent ranches. However, return of the surface rights on these ranches to Navajo ownership did not solve the land problems of the local people, although they undoubtedly felt pride in the tribal action. The land is held in fee simple and the tribe as a corporate entity pays taxes, as would any owner of real estate. The tribe has leased the grazing rights for a number of separate tracts to several individual Navajos, only a few of whom are from local families.

Today, the expansion of mining activities also threatens the homes and rangelands of many of the Chaco Navajos. The mineral rights to the large coal deposits beneath their country are held by the federal government and the railroad, both of which have plans for leasing these rights for strip mining. A people still working to catch up with the education level of the general population now faces possible loss of lands needed to preserve a way of life.

The uncertainties of their tenuous hold on the land, which has persisted for so long, seem destined to remain for some time yet. Question remains as to whether an ultimate resolution of the matter will be found, and if so, whether it will result in acquisition of secure Navajo title. There can be little doubt, however, that with each performance of Blessingway in the eastern Navajo region, prayers are repeated for the return of lands within the domain of the sacred mountains.

David Brugge, an anthropologist and recognized authority on Athapascans in the Southwest, is staff curator for the Southwest Region of the National Park Service. He has written *A History of the Chaco Navajos.*

Suggested Reading

BETANCOURT, JULIO L., AND THOMAS R. VAN DEVENDER
1981   "Holocene Vegetation in Chaco Canyon, New Mexico," *Science* 214: 656–58.

BRUGGE, DAVID M.
1980   "A History of the Chaco Navajos," *Reports of the Chaco Center*, Number 4 (Albuquerque, N.M.: National Park Service, Division of Chaco Research).

CORDELL, LINDA S.
1979   "Prehistory: Eastern Anasazi," in *Handbook of North American Indians*, Vol. 9, *Southwest*, ed. Alfonso Ortiz (Washington, D.C.: Smithsonian Institution).

HAYES, ALDEN C., DAVID M. BRUGGE, AND W. J. JUDGE
1981   "Archaeological Surveys of Chaco Canyon, New Mexico," *Publications in Archaeology 18A: Chaco Canyon Studies* (Washington, D.C.: National Park Service).

JUDD, NEIL M.
1954   "The Material Culture of Pueblo Bonito," *Smithsonian Miscellaneous Collections* 124 (Washington, D.C.).
1964   "The Architecture of Pueblo Bonito," *Smithsonian Miscellaneous Collections* 147(1) (Washington, D.C.).

JUDGE, W. J., WILLIAM B. GILLESPIE, STEPHEN H. LEKSON, AND HENRY W. TOLL
1981   "Tenth Century Developments in Chaco Canyon," in *Collected Papers in Honor of Erik Kellerman Reed*, ed. A. H. Schroeder, *Papers of the Archaeological Society of New Mexico* 6 (Albuquerque).

JUDGE, W. J., AND JOHN D. SCHELBERG, EDS.
1983   "Recent Research in Chacoan Prehistory," *The Kiva* 49:1–2 (Santa Fe, N.M.).

KINCAID, CHRIS, ED.
1983   "Chaco Roads Project, Phase 1: A Reappraisal of Prehistoric Roads in the San Juan Basin 1983" (Albuquerque, N.M.: Bureau of Land Management).

LISTER, ROBERT H., AND FLORENCE C. LISTER
1981   *Chaco Canyon: Archaeology and Archaeologists* (Albuquerque: University of New Mexico Press).

McNITT, FRANK
1957   *Richard Wetherill: Anasazi* (Albuquerque: University of New Mexico Press).

POWERS, ROBERT P., WILLIAM B. GILLESPIE, AND STEPHEN H. LEKSON
1983   "The Outlier Survey: A Regional View of Settlement in the San Juan Basin," *Reports of the Chaco Center*, Number 3 (Albuquerque, N.M.: National Park Service, Division of Chaco Research).

REYMAN, JONATHAN E.
1976   "Astronomy, Architecture, and Adaptation at Pueblo Bonito," *Science* 193:957-62.

SOFAER, ANNA, R. M. SINCLAIR, AND L. E. DOGGETT
1982   "Lunar Markings on Fajada Butte, Chaco Canyon, New Mexico," in
        Archaeoastronomy in the New World, ed. A. F. Aveni (Cambridge,
        England: Cambridge University Press).

VIVIAN, GORDON, AND TOM W. MATTHEWS
1965   "Kin Kletso: A Pueblo III Community in Chaco Canyon, New Mex-
        ico," *Southwestern Monuments Association Technical Series* 6(1) (Globe,
        Arizona).

VIVIAN, R. GWINN, DULCE N. DODGEN, AND GAYLE H. HARTMANN
1978   "Wooden Ritual Artifacts from Chaco Canyon, New Mexico: The
        Chetro Ketl Collection," *Anthropological Papers of the University of Ari-
        zona* 32 (Tucson).

Index

References to illustrations are in italics.